<u>Paint</u>

Shit

𝕽𝖊𝖉

Some see the world black

Others want it white

I Painted Shit Red

So Hot

PAINT SHIT RED Copyright © by Gocni Schindler All rights reserved. No parts of this book may be used or reproduced. In any matter, whatsoever without written permission except in the case of brief quotations embodied in critical articles and reviews.

this work of fiction is intended for someone, might not be you!

For you Sam...

In your passing, my eyes became wide

Seeing the world for the first time

I held you in my arms

Till the blue removed the white

Couldn't save you

I failed as a dad...I'm sorry...

Paint Shit Red

Contents

Wilber's Traveling Carnival Show 1

A Sad Melody 30

Neverland Child 31

Love me... ineffably 33

Remember Me She Whispered 37

A Little Dab'll Do Ya! 41

Notes Don't State 45

Mothers Dish 52

Desensitize Society 57

Farewell Tuna 66

Journal entry: Who cares 71

Mr. Hot Dogger 74

Lip's Pickled Eggs 80

A Ball Crosses the Street 88

Drinking My Pain Away 95

Typical the Standards 101

Jesus Bring the Check 110

I Remember America 118

Water Chestnuts 123

Twas Justice 126

This Bit of Something 132

Writing slipped my mind 134

Shit Writing 139

Hope 153

Expected reject of Expectation 157

Twenty Fourth Hour _1 166

Twenty Fourth Hour_2 169

Twenty Fourth Hour_3 172

Twenty Fourth Hour_4 175

Twenty Fourth Hour_5 176

Twenty Fourth Hour_6 181

The Experience 185

Oblivious to the World Around 199

Going to Buy a House 214

Nothing Wrong with A Little Dreaming

No Love for Self 232

Down with the Middle Finger 236

Café Conversation 242

Walking on no Particular Day 253

She Hulk 259

Condition of My Parole 262

Farewell Night Flyer 266

For on the Morrow They All could be Gone 268

Leaving Nothing to Remain 279

Mommy 281

His Name is Peel 286

Bored as Shit 292

Inverse Lucidity 298

Come Along 308

Gocni Schindler Presents 319

Darkness 327

Toothpaste Via Mail 333

Excellent Productions 341

I Still Write 356

Drink My Sour Milk 363

Weld it Better 374

Raise some Hell 384

Wilber's Traveling Carnival Show

The sun breaks the horizon, welcoming a new day
Roaring down the highway, an Ol'Mac truck
Smoke billows from two tall stacks
Another day, same as the last
Two, the number occupants inside the cab
Gunnin along a dirty back road, leaving behind a line of dust
Side of the rig has a label, that simply reads Wilber's Traveling Carnival
There is a huge pot hole in the road
The rig goes through it while the front bumper makes it a little deeper.
The occupants tossed around a bit inside the rig
Some miles down the road
Outside another small town with small minded individuals
In the County of Poontang, good old US of A
Summertime for the madness
Wilber, pulls the rig into an open field
A balding man, dressed in a fine business suit,
standing by a black Lincoln, he's a bit overweight, smoking a cigar.
The tractor trailer comes to a stop
Dust, elegantly floats turning clean air dirty
The hand on the ignition turns the key
Grumbling the beast goes into silence
Left hand upon the door latch, opening, making a screeching of metal grinding noise
Wilber, looks at the lady in the passenger seat

"Uh, buttercup, augh, no need for ya to get out, this will only take a minute or two."

She just blank stares as if another world.

"Hurry back my Wilber, you know I don't like being alone"

Leaning over Wilber plants a nice kiss on her cheek

"Augh, lickety split my buttercup, lickety split."

Wilber steps down, closing the door.
Now, he's not a well-built creature
Stands about 5'10 walks with a bit of a limp, more of a hobble
left leg shorter than the right, a defect from birth
He's not clean shaven, doesn't really have a beard either,
sporting some tattered blue dickies, he uses a rope for a belt
which causes his ass to hang out
Wearing a flannel shirt that seems to be a walkin corpse
Making his way to the Fat balding man wearing a suit
The fat balding man looks Wilber over, his face tells a tale of
holy shit, what the fuck planet did this retard come from.
Wilber approaches, his face has a half smile and his top lip
extends past the base of his nose, right eye is twitching and his
head has a slight shake as he Extends his hand, introducing
himself.

"Uh, augh, howdy sir, augh, Wilber's the name, someone called about the gig, he he, uh, you hit that pothole in the road? Damn near knocked my buttercup on the floor, oh, augh, goodness."

The Fat balding man with a large cigar pressed between lips
Sucks in, the end of the cigar lights up red, smoke billows
from out of his nostrils
His eyes look at Wilber's hand, while his face wears an
expression of get that fucking hand away from me,
as he raises his gaze to a halfcocked smile upon this human
degenerate. Inhaling once again on that large cigar, letting out
the cloud of smoke towards Wilber's face.
Fat balding man talks with the cigar in his mouth.

"Opposite direction."

Wilber frowns a bit as the guy who's balding and overdressed, scowls.

Not paying anymore mind to the guy's attitude Wilber smiles again

"Uh, that be a mighty, augh nice cigar you have there."

Wilber tilts his head to the side peering at the cigar, half of his teeth are missing, the other half black
as his breath lingers to the fat balding man's nose

"Augh, uh, what, is that, augh, a Miami Rose?"

Two eyes look Wilber cold up and down, eyes visibly reading of disgust with the presence of filth
A fat hand removes the cigar from the mouth

"Article is in the trunk."

Wilber scratches his head a bit, then places his hand back in his pocket. His hand starts jerking
Causing his pants to flutter about as he lets out a satisfactory moan his mouth hangs open and drool
Rolls off his chin as his head lightly shakes.

"Uh, right, augh, ooh, buttercup, ooh, uh, ahhhk, ahhhk, that's the spot."

Stopping Wilber looks at the angered fat balding man who is seething, Wilber puts his hand over his mouth to stop from laughing as he looks down then up again then down. He's cupping a fist as he does the chicken, the child like laughter escapes for a bit.

"Augh, yeah, got me a bad case of dry rot down there, uh, augh, you know what I mean!?

Fat balding man with malcontent shaking his head

"No, I don't!"

Wilber sensing the tension starts shaking his head for yes

Augh, um, uh, take a look see, what goodies y'all have for me."

Wilber's shaken finger pointing in and out like a blinking arrow towards the trunk, fat balding man clicks the key fob. The trunk starts to open, its automatic as Wilber looks it curiously up and down.

"Augh, uh, its magic Ahhhk, ahhhk!"

The Fat balding man places the cigar between his lips, sucks in as the end lights red
Smoke covers his face as he blows it towards Wilber.

"Yes, magic, article is in there.
Tilting his head towards the trunk as he billows more smoke from his nose mumbling under his breath
"You know the expectation."

Rocking back and forth Wilber nods a bit

"Uh, um, expectation, augh, like we discussed my buttercup

Wilber starts to count his fingers

"One, I collect article, Two, I collect payment Three I remove the article. Four"

The fat balding man rudely almost nonlover like, interjects

"Look hook, I am not your buttercup, got it!

Poking his finger in Wilber's chest. Wilber giggles making the fat balding man even more angered and then suddenly his face cracks a smile.

"You do what we tell you or it turns out very bad for you!"

Cracking his knuckles the fat balding man laughs

"Very bad!"

Wilber's head shakes as he wears a shit grinning smile. Fat balding man can see clearly, he's dealing with someone four cans short of a six pack.

"uh, looksee, looksee what we got here, augh, well, ahhhk, two, payment, ahhhk, ahhhk, we'll be on our way."

Taking another pull from the cigar blowing smoke directly in Wilber's face
One hand reaches inside his suit jacket, pulling out a manila envelope
Grimacing, coughing, Wilber begins waving his hand in front of his face to remove the lingering smoke
Eyes twitching as his other hand grabs to take the envelope. Pulling the Fat balding man doesn't let it go

"Uh, let me, augh, just take this ahhhk, ahhhk, we'll be on our way, lickety split."

Two hands upon an envelope stuck in a game of grab and release
Removing the cigar once again from between the lips

"You know what happens if this doesn't get finished?'

Releasing the envelope sending Wilber skidding back on wobbly knees. Shaking his head while placing the envelope down his pants

"Uh, yesses, we know what happens, y'all want a refund, excuse me, while I grab this here, let me get this article."

The Fat balding man moves aside while he eyeballs Wilber

"Will be more than just a fuckin refund pal."

5

Wilber reaches inside the trunk awkwardly trying to lift, pulling a large item wrapped in a what could be labeled as a bed sheet. The nature of things causes it to crash to the floor for Wilber isn't the strongest of men. It makes a thud as a part of it comes out. Fat balding man angrily looks at Wilber then down at the article. Wilber shakes his head as he lets out a laugh

"Augh, woooopsie pooopsie daddy, tuck that in like, all's best uh uh."

Scratching his ass, pulling up his pants Wilber tries again

"uh, augh, this heavy, y'all said buck fifty? Feels two fifty-three and sweat from ahhk, Aunt Helga's ball sack."

Fat balding man still shaking his head while dropping the butt of the cigar to the ground. A nicely polished Italian style shoe grinds it into the earth as he looks towards the cigar being ground into soil, his eyes flash up, looking at Wilber. All he can think about is why he hasn't shot this insect and did the world a favor. But he understands, in this instance, that he needs this type of retard scum. Though, the mental strain has gotten the best of him

"My employers said you're a professional, all I see is a retarded slob."

With his hand on the article Wilber glances up and he isn't taking the comment to kindly

"Augh, now, now, ahhhk, you shouldn't, ahhhk, shouldn't have said it, no sir, buttercup, buttercup doesn't like it when people call me that word, no, augh, no sir, that ahhhk, word is vile, forbidden for us to use augh, uh huh."

Wilber begins to drag the article while still speaking outload

"No sir, don't you call me it, don't you speak it naughty ahhhk, ahhhk, buttercup, naughty ahhhk ."

6

Dragging the article across the ground Wilber grinds his remaining teeth together, his eye twitches as a tear is released With his hand on the trunk the fat balding man pushes it closed

"Who you speaking to fucking retard?"

Reaching the back of the trailer, Wilber lifts on the metal bars and opens the massive trailer door.
Bending down he grabs the article and with some grunting and groaning his face is stretched from the straining. With all his strength, lifting with that old heave ho might, it goes up and quickly throws his shoulder into it making a grunting, groaning, as his legs shake, finally, the article is loaded. The black silhouette stuffed between the sidewall and the wood secure rail catches his eye. With an upward motion of his arm, he releases it from the location, cold in his hand, cold black steel. Wilber's eyes frantically gaze upon it, as his hand strokes it gently, in a loving fashion, huge the baby smile crosses his face exposing a mouth of blacken rot.

"Uh, augh, my sweet pea, so lovely, ahhhk, my wonderful, wonderful lovely."

Wilber places his lips to the cold steel, licking the metal, kissing it, stroking the perfect curve

"Uh, my sweet pea, help me wonderfully will, yes, yes will.

Wilber kisses it another time holding high it in front of him. So much so, with a great joy in his eye
The fat balding man pulls out his cell, begins a texting message

"Article's delivered! Where did you find this fucking retard? Christ it's disgusting"

Wilber, contemplates the scenario in his head, all the possibilities, his eyebrow raises and lowers as his closed mouth moves around like it's trying to speak

"Augh, ahhhk, punished, my buttercup, called me naughty vile word, What's that my buttercup? What's that? Yes, augh, yes, ahhhk, I have my sweet pea, its hear, comforts me, that vile word we not speak, Ahhhk."

Chirp, chirp, the fat balding man's phone blasts away
Reading the message

"Boss found him on the want ads on Craigslist, he gets the job done. The boss wants you to head back.
Another client is refusing to pay for services rendered
They need you to make a political contribution"

Two fat thumbs type a response of "Heading back now"
as he speaks out for Wilber to hear

"Hey retard, you done? I need to leave."

Those words, words, that simply sail through the air like lightning. Crashing into Wilber's ear
Retard, it just rolls around his mind like a marble circling an empty Ball jar, faster and faster it goes till finally, the Ball jar breaks, setting the marble free. Wilber's mouth bunches together as the corners lower and the middle raises. Those eyebrows burrow deep as his body starts trembling, tightening his ass cheeks hips thrusting forwards then backwards.

"Augh, yes buttercup, he called me that word, ahhhk, nasty, nasty man for speakin it to me, do him dirty my buttercup, ahhhk, dirty we do him."

With an open hand, Wilber begins to slap himself as his eyes wet with tears

"Uh, stop it, augh, I'm not, ahhhk, I'm not, I'm not, stop it, I'm not, that dirty word!"

The word, so simplistic changes things, the circuit board shorts out. Wilber's eye twitches

"I am not, my buttercup, I am not, that vile word not permitted."

With that hobbling strut, his head halfcocked to the left, eyes twitching and a black metal object in his hand that he's using to scratch his head.

"Augh, um, excuse me, you say to me?"

The fat balding man looks up from his phone. His eyes perceive what is in Wilber's hand, some call it a wrecking bar, others might label it a crowbar. For a moment, he thinks the worst. Then he looks Wilber in the eyes and finds some innocent assurance he wouldn't dare it, he doesn't have the balls, for Christ sake the guys a retard

"What?"

Wilber grimaces almost squirrel like, just a little

"Augh, um, said something, didn't ya? Ahhk, uh huh, to me ya did, when I was putting article away. What did you say? ahhhk I heard ya, augh, don't play fool with me!"

A smile forms on the fat balding man's face, its created from the inward comedy of what he deems lesser in life, Wilber this human scum of retardation

"I asked if we are done here, retard, so, are we, done?"

Wilber lets out a sigh of relief, then laughs as he puts his hands on his knee

"augh, buttercup the chicken scratch. Ahhhk, Yesses, chicken scratch, moment ago, I heard it my buttercup, chicken scratch."

Shaking his head the fat balding man opens the car door turning to get into the car

"Fucking retard, you have some serious issues."

Wilber lifts his hand, that one simple hand that holds the metal object, his eye twitches as he smirks

"Augh, uh-huh, one thing."

The fat balding man annoyed turns to face Wilber

"Jesus Christ for fucks sake retard."

The final message and Wilber plows the black metallic object into the fat balding man's head. A mist of rainbow juice sprays red into the air. Wilber's eyes, wide, smiles with deep content. A grunt protrudes from the fat balding man's mouth as he stumbles back into the opening of the car door. That section that makes a nice V, between the car door and the frame. Anger races across his face, he's a big man, no one dares to ever attempt this

"You're a dead meat stick retard."

Wilber just sees a new world; the fat balding man's screams are never heard. Magically Wilber is set in a new frame laughing joyously all the way as Teddy the unicorn, showing himself within the cage of fat balding man's skull. Teddy's innocent eyes just look so helpless towards Wilber.

"Wilber, help me, I'm trapped, the evil has me locked away in this cage."

Wilber looks on in shock, all surreal now, this new time makes sense. Placing his hand on his hip leaning forward, head tilted towards the side

"augh, Teddy, uh, ahhhk, now how ya get in there, inside that evil cage?"

Eyes, big blue eyes, tear filled eyes, Teddy the Unicorn tears rain red as the drips hit the ground causing colorful candy to start growing

"He's taken me hostage Wilber violating me day and night, Oh, Wilber, he's violating, help me."

The fat balding man wipes the blood from his face with his hand, Wilber just looks on in a daze from his talk with Teddy, the droplets of blood hit the earth. Reaching into his suit jacket, removing a silver gun from the holster. Wilber is having some conversation calling out to Teddy

"Who the fuck is Teddy retard? Time to say goodnight motherfucker!"

The gun comes out, heading towards Wilber's head.

"Wilber, Wilber get me out of this cage."

Wilber shaking his head

"Augh, yes, ahhhk, yes Teddy."

The metal object, some call it at wrecking bar, others call it a crowbar. For Wilber, it's just an object he calls sweet pea, which so happens to fit comfortably in his hand. Wilber arch's it downward violently, no thought, no contemplation, just a wide-eyed smile. The bar meeting the fat balding man's arm. The cracking noise, like a large stick, breaking over the knee. The gun blasts, the bullet ricocheted off the face of mother earth. The fat balding man screaming in agony, seeing his ulna bone protruding from the skin. Once again, knocked back into that V where the door and the car frame meet. The gun bouncing on the ground.
Wilber looks down, tilting his head to the left as his chin extends out a little bit, pointing sweet pea at the fat balding man

"Um, augh, don't worry ahhhk, Teddy, I'll get you out, lickety split."

The fat balding man with fuming fear, sporadically using his foot, attempting to slide the gun over to his other hand as his eyes race in terror from the vile instrument in Wilber's hand

"Who the fuck is Teddy you god damn retard, what the hell is wrong with you!"

Wilber looking down at the vile fat balding man, with a gaze so blank you could see through the other side and discover no one is home

"Uh, um, ya viler, kidnapped Teddy, kept him, violated him! Told me so he did, goin ta set him, augh, ahhhk, free!"

The foot of the fat balding man connects with the gun, sending it sliding to his other hand. The finger slides into the hole as he starts to lift it up wanting to gun down Wilber dead.
Down comes Wilber's hand, sinking the claw of the bar into the fat balding man's head. Fat balding man's eyes look upward at the crowbar protruding from his skull. Two fat legs start to shake as his finger on the trigger squeezes off two more rounds. Blasts echo through the field as Wilber leans in on the bar, air escaping the fat balding man's mouth as his body convulses.

"augh, I'm comin Teddy, ahhhk, hang in there, augh buddy, I'm a comin, outta that nasty."

Placing his foot on the chest of the fallen fat balding man, with all his might, lifts on the bar
Tears of pain, of joy, flowing from Wilber's eye, as he joyfully laughs and moans from all the torquing. Cracking sound, as a large chunk of skull is ripped away
The release sends Wilber falling backwards towards the ground. In complete amazement, a funnel of rainbow is sprayed into the air. Teddy is gasping, getting Wilber extra

excited, launching back upon his feet smiling and happy to free his friend

"Uh, augh, hold on Teddy, ahhhk uh, have you out, jiffy."

Raising the bar high, held with both hands, his eyes a bit cross as he starts jumping while he swings away in a rage
Each swing, plummeting deeper into the skull. Rainbow juice and chunks of sugar cane spraying all over the place, finally, Teddy is released, the white unicorn mightily stepping out, shaking the rainbow juice away

"You did it Wilber! You saved me."

Wilber, adjusting his pants, removes a hanky from his back pocket wiping away the red juice from his face
Pulling up on his pants that suddenly fell towards his knees, the envelope falls down the pants leg,
He's digging down trying to pull it up

"Um, augh, ya safe now Teddy ahhhk."

Looking down towards the former cage Teddy smiles at Wilber.

"Thank you again, friend, you saved me."

Pointing his hoof towards the fat balding man's corpse

"Please, Wilber, help yourself to the candy from this newly opened bowl. My love, I freely give this gift with my sincerest appreciation."

Wilber smiling, reaches down, grabbing a handful of the juicy sugar plumps from the opened bowl.

"Augh, um, thank ya for given me a treatsy weepsy."

Teddy, lifting his head high, his horn glistening silver, blue and purple from the sun's rays.

Wilber places the juicy sugar plumps in his mouth and begins to chew, the juices drip from his mouth as he looks at Teddy with a childlike smile that would make any parent proud.

Teddy places his hoof on Wilber's shoulder looking him clear in the eye

"Wilber, you're not a retard, let no one speak that vile word, you're my special needs, I made you special and I AM the light that saves the world."

Wilber, shaking his head as he sticks another handful of juicy sugar plumps into his mouth. Chewing as his eyes roll savoring the flavor, then abruptly stops, as a hard piece of sugar sticks him in the gum. Reaching, digging his fingers around inside his mouth, his eyes, look upwards, as his eyebrows raise, he pulls it out, looks at its odd rough shape, frowns and shrugs his shoulders then tosses it to the ground. Continues chewing and slurping as the juices and chunks fall from his chin and lips.

"Uh, augh, Yes Teddy, we don't allow that vile word, Ahhhk, my buttercup tells me."

Teddy looks Wilber in the eye one last time

"Good Wilber, good, I'm off to the free world, enjoy, my gift of candy my child."

Teddy runs off into the invisible realm, Wilber fills his mouth again as he waves goodbye trying to speak with a mouth full.

"Augh, I'll enjoy this candy, ahhhk, so much, bye Teddy, bye."

Wilber watches as Teddy departs back to where he belongs. Safe and sound.

Hobbling back to the rig, a juicy bloody left hand grabs the latch opening the door. Wilber steps up and looks at his precious buttercup.

"Augh, um, sorry my buttercup, Teddy was locked away in that nasties cage but look he gave us treatsy weepsy."

Wilber smiling and happy, places some juicy sugar plumps into her hand.

"What took you so long Wilber?"

Grabbing a towel between the seat Wilber starts to wipe the red away while licking his fingers clean.

"Um, augh, ahhhk, ahhhk that nasty, said bad words to me my buttercup, called me what we don't speak."

Her emotionless gaze is fixed straight

"Did you teach him a lesson my Wilber? Teach him not to use those dirty words?"

Wilber looking up

"Um, I sure did, augh, Teddy was captive, ahhhk, set Teddy free, we did, from that nasty."

Wilber finishes cleaning himself

"Augh, be right back my buttercup, lickety-split, ahhhk we will."

Wilber leans over the captain's chair and kisses his buttercup on the cheek, her head hangs low

"Hurry my Wilber I'm so alone."

Shaking his head

"augh, yes, my buttercup, yes. Um, augh, right quick."

Sliding back out of the cab to the ground, he closes the door and wipes the blood from the handle
Hobbling back over to the Lincoln where the fat balding man's corpse is resting, between the door and frame of the car. The earth is enjoying the feast of blood. Scratching his head Wilber contemplates what to do. Reaching down, pulls the wrecking bar from what remains of the former fat balding man's skull.
Picking up the shiny gun and placing it in the back of his trousers. His pants start to fall, he starts a wild commotion fighting the air, mumbling as he pulls his pants back up and reties the rope belt tight

"Uh, augh, told naughty, not to use those vile words. kept Teddy hostage, learned ya lesson we did, Teddy made me special, you don't talk that way, my buttercup and sweet pea done tell, tell ya no, no ya don't use bad word."

Grabbing the feet Wilber begins to drag the fat balding man to the back of the trailer.

Twenty minutes' prior
Cruising down the lost highway, a brown and gold squad car.
The star on the door states: Poontang County Sherriff
A crucifix dangles from the review mirror. A Hawaiian dancer bounces on the dash
Above the CB radio is a picture of a wife figure and some piss and shit kids
No one in the picture is smiling, just frowns
The scenery is your average poo dung trailer trash country meadow location
An Occasional barn here and there, the typical sites of shit from yesteryears.
Uncle Tom's bull is climbing on a heifer banging one away
A deputy driving, looking at all the same shit day in, day out
His eyes have bags under them, a little dark in color
Somehow, a double chin appeared, grew as the years disappeared

His hand, white knuckling the steering wheel. Not from fear of driving
Just the anger of not achieving much

"Nothing ever happens here! Nothing!"

Some old nag is heard on the radio calling for car number six-sixty-six. A hand halfway to death removes itself from the steering wheel picking up the CB Mic
A disgruntled voice is spoken into the Mic

"Car six-sixty-six, over!"

A raspy woman's voice like she's been chain smoking for twenty years is heard crackling through the receiver.

"Hey deputy, we have reports of a code 82, those lot lizards at Earl's Truck and Dine again. The Sherriff wants you to head over to investigate."

Looking out the window shaking his head

"Affirmative, car six heading to Earl's to investigate the 82 car six-sixty-six over and out."

Placing the mic back into its holster

"Deputy dip shit, go check out the lot lizards at that drug stop, Earl should just put beds up in there, not like this changes anything, fucking truckers need a little loving and this shit is just natural selection."

The deputy reaches down and lifts the cup of hot coffee from the holder between the seats.

"Swear this place is a living hell, nothing interesting, other than chasing prostitutes away from that shit hole truck stop."

As he's looking down, so that he doesn't burn his lip from the hot liquid, he doesn't see the massive pot hole in the highway.

The front tire hits the hole bouncing the car up like a rocket, sending the coffee cup free sailing, hitting the roof and smashing into the dash, the lid explodes off, while the contents of hot liquid fall all over the CB and the deputy. The CB starts to spark. The deputy loses hold of the steering wheel as the car skids left to right, the deputy is trying to maintain control while holding his shirt away from his chest as its burning. The CB starts making a gurgling noise and black smoke fills the cab of the car. The deputy starts to cough as he starts to regain control of the car. Cussing and screaming as the car is skidding and sliding. Left hand rolling down the window, letting the smoke out as the deputy locks up the breaks, sending the car to an abrupt halt.
Getting out of the car, the deputy puts his hand out wide and surveys his uniform. the warm liquid is suddenly turning cold. Reaching in for his cell that is swimming inside the cup holder now full of coffee.

"Fucking great, just great, fuck you, you mother fucker!"

As he looks at the cell it just repeatedly flashes. The lights on the CB are dead. He throws the cell phone inside the car like a baseball
Walking over to survey the massive hole in the dirt road. Scratching his noggin, he proceeds to the trunk of the cruiser, unlocking and pulling out a road cone.
Placing it in front of the massive hole to prevent a major accident.
Doing the duty of serving and protecting the good people he swore an oath to.
Getting back into the squad car, adjusts the mirror. Looks down at the CB radio, picking up the mic starts hitting it against the dash breaking it in his hand. Ripping the cord away he tosses the Mic out the window. Putting the car in drive, strolls down the road towards Earls. The steering wheel is a bit cocked to the right and the front end is making an unusual grinding, sending vibrations through the car

'Sure, hope this piece of shit makes it or else going to be a long walk back to that shit hole station."

Just another day, ordinary, like every other day. That is what used to run through the deputy's brain. Now, he is wet and pissed and the tension builds as he limps along this vast empty roadway

The tree line is a bit long, then the opening and as the deputy looks beyond, his mind thinks on how that's odd to see a black Lincoln and a tractor trailer parked in good old farmer Oats empty field. It doesn't register at first. How could it, when shits always the same, day in, day out, the same. The way he feels right now, after one simple hole destroys his world. He watches as a man, hobbling while dragging another man to the back of that trailer.

"This shit can't be happening, can it? Did I hit my head from that pot hole"?

One of those questions, out of the blue type, the deputy has found himself asking. He reluctantly closes his eyes only to open them seeing the same that he saw before he closed them

"Shit's happening, he's dragging that body to the back of his trailer."

His voice is giddy, filled with anticipation and excitement. The rush of blood sends a good vibe to his brain

"Yes, finally, finally fucking something real, something worth my while."

A miracle just took place, here is this out of the ordinary event. To hell with going to Earls to handle the lot lizards again. To hell with this small-town mediocrity, here is a real fucking case. The deputy, out of instinct, reaches down to call it in. Then it dawns on him, he remembers, that he has no communications. He will be on his own. Giving himself the pep talk

"This is what we train for maggot, the time is now, time to do this officer."

He flips the lights and wheels in to the empty lot of land

Current Time

As Wilber is draggin the body, of that fat balding man, to the back of the trailer. He hears this odd noise, grinding, chirpin and squealing followed by sirens and flashy lights. Looking up, he sees the cop car, Panic, sets in as he looks to his right and left. His body is shaking, he's talking to himself, looking for some help, Teddy is nowhere to be found. His buttercup is in the cab. Sweet pea is on the ground. The lights and sirens go off as the cruiser pulls into the open lot.

"Uh, um shit, augh run, ahhhk run, hide retard!"

Slapping himself across the face his eyes look away from his hand.

"Uh, ahhhk no look at it, forbidden vile word, run Ahhhk, ahhhk

Wilber starts to move right, the cruiser hard on the gas is pulling up in that very direction. Wilber turns again, then goes left about two steps then turns towards the right and spins on his heel to the left again. From the deputy perspective, it would appear, that this guy is doing some form of dance. Locking up the breaks on the car, it skids a bit to the left on open dirt, slamming the shifter into park gears grind as it abruptly stops. Opening the door, the deputy attempts to get out, then gets caught by the seatbelt he forgot about. He's cursing, saying things like God dammit, shit, fuck, cocksucker and the like! Finally, he protrudes from the car door while attempting to draw his gun. His face has excitement and panic written well upon it like he's fifty shades of something.

"Freeze mother fucker!"

The easiest words flow off the deputy's tongue

Wilber makes it around the corner, hiding by the rear tires. He's shaking, a wave of panic rolls over him

"Uh, um, augh, I'm scared, Wilber, me too, I'm scared too. Augh, ahhhk, um, what we going to do?"

The deputy heads towards the front of his car, surveys the body on the ground, reaching towards the neck of the fallen victim, checking for vitals, the basics, instincts taking place, he wasn't prepared for what he'd see.

"Christ, deputy, he's missing most of his head, you think he's alive still dumbass!"

They don't train for this. The fat formerly balding man, missing half his head, his right eye, dangling past his mouth, it's inevitable when mixed with the stench, viewing a human being that has a head which more resembles an exploded mushroom. It dawns on him, his eyes see it but as it is with scenarios like this the mind blocks certain things, though his training pushes past the normal mental fears. His mind now understands, that the inner parts where ripped out by hand. The vomiting, wasn't part of the planning, he's always been a good officer, so he thought. Was a man raised by a man Daddy never let the boys cry, they must be men, here he is puking like a little pansy. His dad would have kicked him in the nut sack if he was still around. He needs to understand he's a man. He just wasn't--strong enough. Coffee mixed with Mrs. Watts famous cakes, followed by a mushy red substance, from the seeds you could see it was the strawberries he had on his pancakes.

"Oh, god, oh, god, what is going on here? This doesn't happen here!"

The deputy regains some mental ground as he leans on the back side of his car. Clicking the mic on his portable. It's just unfortunate that its connected to the device in the car that has been destroyed. He slams it down

"Fuck, fuck, fuck! Think god dammit, think!"

Composing himself he thunders

"Alright, now, come out here, with your hands up, nice and easy, get on your knees with your face down and this will all go smoothly, you understand? I need to know you understand, answer me, we have you surrounded!"

Silence, eternal in scope, Wilber eyes franticly searching for an exit, quietly slides towards the front of the truck, looking underneath he sees the deputy's feet and a calm comes over him for he knows the officer is alone.

"Wilber, the cop is screamin at us? What are we going to do?"

Wilber waddles back and forth digging his fists into his eyes, he slaps himself hard,

"Ahhhk, Wilber is naughty, getting caughty."

Shaking his head violently while bunching up his nose

"Augh, uh, no, it doesn't speak, ahhhk, it's quiet, gammy said its quiet, its quiet, quiet ahhhk, ahhhk."

Then, as it is the words of the deputy start to sink and Wilber pulls the gun from out of his back.

"Wilber, what we gonna do?"

Wilber looks at the gun, three, the bullets that remain. He bites his lip as his hand shakes

"Augh, uh, don't you fret my buttercup, gonna make it all better gotta save sweet pea."

The deputy moves towards the back of the trailer. The door still open. Pulling out his gun, flashlight, proceeds to check the interior. Back and forth checking all corners
The article rolled in what would be considered nothing more than bed sheets.
Shining the light inside the darkened space
Racks along the walls, drying racks, down the center, swinging meat hooks
Towards the front, one giant freezer, from ceiling to floor and wall to wall
Looking closer, something is hanging from the hooks
The flashlight starts flickering and out it goes,

"God dammit these pieces of shit lights, I told the sheriff to order the high-quality, fuckers always trying to go cheap, purchasing these Made in China piece of shits, no wonder it keeps breaking"

Smashing the light against his hand, it comes on again, as he aims it towards the center
The rolled article, in the bed sheets starts to shake and squirm
The motion startles the deputy as he drops his flashlight frantically aiming his gun at the moving thing One trembling hand reaching towards the top of the rolled bed sheets, with his gun pointed, pulls down on the sheets.
Two big black eyes, look out, The deputy in horror as anger rolls across his face

"What is this in my county, no, no, not in my county, not on my watch!

Walking towards the corner that Wilber ran around

" I told you god dammit, come out now, with your damn hands up and I promise you, no harm will come to you. If you don't comply by the count of three we're coming to get you. One, Two, last warning mother fucker!"

Front of the rig, Wilber scratching his head, contemplates which path to take by pointing his fingers, sticking a finger up

his nose it digs around pulling out a long stringed booger as he is looking up, he sees his buttercup looking back at him, a sincere frown comes across his mouth as he inserts the snot into his mouth. Knowing what he must do. The ramblings of the deputy, heard with both ears.
He must act quickly the officer starts to count.
"One, two, last warning…motherfucker…God dammit…three!

"Wilber, what are we going to do?"

Quietly hobbling down the left side of the tractor trailer crouching by the rigs rear wheels Wilber states his plan. Wilber hacks and coughs a bit

"Uh, um, augh, going to have to exterminate, ahhhk, the nasty."

The deputy on the right corner where Wilber ran, his gun in the air. Like they taught in the academy, in the military. Jumping out, the gun out in front as he searches for the perp. Looking under the trailer, nothing is there.
Wilber on the opposite side shimming along the top of the trailer, reaching the rear door and sliding down. Crawling under the trailer Wilber comes behind the deputy, pulling out the gun from his trousers, taking aim at the deputy.

"Augh, time to go night, night ahhhk, ahhhk."

Wilber squeezes the trigger and it goes click. With a face, full of dumbfound, starts smacking the gun with his hand, looking down the barrel, making some grumbling noises, smacking the gun.
Click was the unmistaken noise, Deputy hears it at the gun range every Sunday afternoon, when he goes shooting with the boys.
Hearing the sound, the deputy's breath escapes as the heart races. He lunges forward.
Wilber squeezes the trigger and the gun fires, he screams as the bullet shoots into the trailer and bounces around.

The deputy crawling towards the tires for cover, mere feet from him, safety is what crosses his mind. Wilber aims the gun and fires a round, blazing forward, the nasty bullet blasts through the deputies left heel and into his right leg. Blood curdling screams rage, from his vocal cords, no sound on earth can duplicate. The deputy, once again, that instinct, aiming his gun in the vicinity where the noise was heard, starts shooting his gun sporadically as he tries to crawl. Wilber, with a big smile as the deputy is struck with the bullet, the smile is short lived, its wiped clear off his face as he watches the deputy swing the gun directly towards his direction.

"Ahhhk, augh, no my buttercup"

The bullets hit above him, beside him, as the dirt explodes. Wilber rolls away. The deputy in agony looking, sees Wilber getting up as he starts to hobble. From nowhere an explosion blows through Wilber's arm. Blood sprays through the air as the impact has him spun around as he goes crashing to the ground.
His eyes, frantically look at his arm, he slaps the gunshot wound, as he screams away in agony. The deputy grabbing the top of the rear tire tries to pull himself up, groans as he leans his chest against the tire. The pain, shooting through his legs, his eyes rolling in the back of his head. Looking up, spotting Wilber rolling on the ground brings him great joy.

"Take that you mother fucker."

The deputy lifting his arm, takes aim, squeezes the trigger, the bullet misses Wilber's face by less than an inch. Wilber in a panic, the deputy and he make a moment of eye contact, eye contact between a predator and its prey, the deputy, shaking his head,

"Don't you do it son of a bitch, don't even dare!"

Wilber, holding his arm, groans and there it is, right in front of him

"Augh, ahhhk, uh my sweet pea, there ya are."

A smile crosses Wilber's face as he grabs his sweet pea and makes a break for it. The deputy fires his entire clip only to miss, the exertion sends him to the ground again in agony and despair. Wilber reaches the door of the cab. His head rubbing the door he looks up placing his hand on the latch, turning, begins to open it. Jumping up into the cab, his face plants into the captain's seat, setting sweet pea between the seats, mustering up the strength to turn his body. Streaks of blood on dirty tan leather Lifting his legs, his good hand secures the door. Those eyes race back and forth as he starts to cry, smashing his fist into his leg.
Turning, he looks at his buttercup, whimpers wanting it to go away

"Ahhk, ahhhk, augh, uh-huh my buttercup, in trouble, hurting, ahhhk help me."

The voice from his angel is soft and comforting

"Wilber start the truck, we must leave!"

Wilber's fingers shake, as his arm raises and his index finger pushes through his hair
His eye twitches, head shakes, reaching over with his good arm he turns the ignition.

"Augh, we're leaving my buttercup, we're leaving, lickety, ahhhk, ahhhk split."

The deputy on the ground, hears Wilber get into the cab. Crawling, on the ground, towards the passenger door.

"This shit doesn't happen on my watch, no way, no way you're getting away."

Adrenaline has the deputy crawling, vengeance, justice, the only medicine he's using to push past reality.

His hand, reaching the running board, attempting, trying, survival, instinct all the things to keep one going. Needing to grab the tank strap, to stand, his hand slips, sending the officer crashing to the ground Pain shoots through his legs as he groans, biting down hard on his teeth, the force cracking one, blood flows from his mouth, though he doesn't notice pain. He's a man's man. With rage, he reaches again, grabbing the strap, pulling himself up. His eye on the latch, reaching it securely. Pulling his feet onto the step, adjusting to alleviate the pain. The doors locked. He sees the shadow of a person in the passenger seat. Checking his bullets in his gun, its empty, reaching for another clip, his side pouch, empty, the extra clip is in the squad car. His fist clench, he wants to scream, punch something, he must restrain

"Fuck me, are you joking!"

The deputy looks up into the mirror, spotting Wilber, sitting in the driver's seat, holding his arm, but his mind doesn't quite understand. It doesn't add up, who is in the passenger seat. He looks again, his face in shock, he looks to heaven, shaking his head as his mind just can't grasp this

"This has to prove there is no god, no god would allow this."

The rig comes to life, the rattle makes the deputy lose a footing, dangling, struggling to hang onto the review mirror. He's crying in agony.

"Christ, fuck me, give me a break here, I need to arrest you!"

Wilber pushes down on the clutch, with his good hand jams the stick into gear. At first, it makes a grinding noise then goes in. One foot presses the gas while the other releases the clutch. The rig bounces forward. The deputy is out of time, he looks down at the butt of his gun.

"This is what I need to do!"

As the truck jerks forward, Wilber takes a clear pouch, holding white powder from the center console and empties the contents into his mouth. His eyes blaze a new blue, the pain instantly removed. He feels invincible. His arm works again. The Rig juts forward, when suddenly glass explodes inside the cab. Wilber smashes down on the gas as the steering wheel turned in the direction of avoiding the glass. The deputy, reaching in, grabbing a body that's light as a feather, not supporting his weight, things are starting to tear away. Thread worn thin from all those years. Wilber, adjusting, he views hell, witnessing the horrific event. His buttercup's in danger and he's focused. The deputy frantically trying to secure a grip. Wilber's hand frantically reaching for sweat pea.

"Ahhhk, augh, uh sweet pea, augh, sweet pea. Don't you hurt my buttercup fartsniffer! Ahhhk, gonna teach you, sweet pea will, ya don't hurt my buttercup!"

The hand, its oddly strong when its life or death, gripping tight, pulling up
The strike, shatters bone,
The deputy screams out as he starts to fall ripping the head off buttercup.
Wilber in absolute horror screams his eyes wide as the moon, protruding from his skull as his jaw hits the floor.

"Ahhhk, augh, AHHHHK, Not my buttercup, nasty lit officer, uh no, my buttercup, no!"

The deputy hits the ground hard, rolling away followed by a bouncing head from this side of weird.
Wilber drives, continually looking at his buttercup who's now headless

"Augh, uh, ya OK my buttercup, we're going to save, we're going to save. Fix you up we will, Wilber fix"

As the semi bounces through the field at a high rate of speed, the article wrapped up in nothing more than bed sheets, bounces out, falling to the ground. Rolling and squirming.

The deputy tries to sit up as the semi hits the dirt road at a high rate of speed.

His eyes, just follow it till he can't see it anymore.

"How the hell am I going to write this one up, was under fire from some fuck that's chopping up humans and making jerky out of them or god knows what."

Reaching over the deputy grabs the mummified head. Looking at what used to be a living human. It has big blue buttons for eyes. The skin is stitched. The hair is long and black, a female from the facial features.

"And who the hell might you be?"

The question rolls inside his mind as he looks at a stuffed human being, that we all know only as buttercup. His eyes are blurry but the deputy views one last thing. At the end of Oats field, a tall figure, had to be at least 8 feet tall, naked, skin, a pale white. running off and disappearing into the tree line.

The film ends

A Sad Melody

As the sun was setting

A white dress was dancing

Through an empty field

All that I heard

Played by the red devil

A soft piano melody

Carefree as she twirled

The ghost was of innocence

Her Poetry was for love

She wailed it from another world

Love, something she never found

The woman in white

Stated the town folk

Her story was suicide

After being left at the alter

Her heart went off with another

Now she is left roaming

Lost to the chorus of degenerates

Her eternity

Dancing to a sad melody

Neverland Child

Let's go on a walk states the father

Into Neverland

Neverland

Run upon this path towards that sacred underworld

Neverland child

Into the underworld

Hither to me, dear innocent, rest thy soul

Nestled close

My beautiful close thine eyes

Wide eyed wonderer look, light breaks the horizon

Darkness fades

Awaken renewed with spiritual wings of vivacity

Fly with me child to a summer eternal

Purities flower

Behold my garden, take and feast this golden fruit

Survey thy glimmering moonbeams within the great mystery

Radiant life

Dear one, partake in this loving frequency

Shimmering star, present yourself, to a beholding servant

Illuminated light

My lover, take this hand

Venture with me, into the white river ethereal

Neverland child

Into the underworld

What is written is hidden

What is hidden is written

Love me... ineffably

I have five minutes

Less than five now

Every wasted stroke

Attempting to pin down a point

What is point?

Living inside a never-ending circle

While delivering some relieving joy

That by reading this

An experience to emotion will be fulfilled

Be it laughter?

Perhaps my dearest

That individual out there

Can't muster the courage to obtain

Needles injected into the brain

Getting off from pain

Beatific, Indescribable

The high

This life

Mine, a putrid comedy of pathetic

Perhaps another great tragedy

Expressing by knowing the experience

Everyone goes through a trial of hell

Lucky the ones that never escape

So, dear child, wipe that eye dry

No longer hide

Hardships befall the whole of mankind

Those pesky crutches

So many to get snared upon

Sadness

Doesn't keep company

My time, this time, I've been deceived

Own it, I do not

Slipping away

Heading to my rot

Cost of thought

Price tag, completely insane

Wanting, I've been uncovered

Passion, though my passion

Unnoticed

The performer, be I, in the corner

Facing the wall

Perishing from hunger

Hidden well by curtains of steel

Moans to the world around

Oh, hear me great gods

My voice triumphant

Give ear, to this being of nothing

Tis I, that doeth hide behind fear

Put arrow to bow

Draw, then loose

Paint me, a sky, misty gray

Label it spotless

Float down to me that veil

Till I feast, allow I... Succumbing

I've only got but a minute

Time, have I not to sell

Sun rises all the same

Nothing of worth

Few shitty words

Written within a portion

The gods will laugh

As I set my value to a scale pan

Then, so it is

In the moment of understanding

Shit, was I made

From poor man's clay

Shit, will I remain

Married

Into thy darkness, matching my blackness

Adorning such classlessness

Dare I, not wear... White

Exposing innocence

For innocence, none have I

Give me cigarettes

Allow me to smoke my fill

Removing unnecessary necessities

Wick of my candle

Almost to an end

Time around the bend

Seconds until it ends

Homeward

It's alright, friend!

Wish the world my very best

Love me... Ineffably

When we stop moving, is when we start dying

Remember Me, She Whispered

Remember whispered the soft voice

Remember me as she slipped into night

Those eyes

Eyes, within a fog

Life beholding no more

Tears running hard

Such a little guy

Talons, talons delivering fear

It was

What was it again?

That made this of worth?

Wind in my face

While my hair flows

As the Air blows

Cruising, down a highway

On my lady

Her name is old

She a good ride

Heart pounding fun

That's all of nothing

What was it again?

That made this of worth?

It was

Skipping down the sidewalk

Smiling at those around

Whistling some new-found song

Enjoying the sun

Listing to the great nothing

Truly, it speaks in abundance

No one stops to hear

Ssshh

Silently be silent

Hear your heartbeat

Resting silence

A whispering upon the wind

Listen

Resonating Speech

That made this of worth

It was

What was it again?

Enjoying greatest of company

A wonderful lady

Soft and compassionate

Endearing

Educated thinker

Encompassing elegance

Beautiful

Throughout the universe of her

Twas a birthday

On no ordinary day

The tenth day past the first

Month of twelve minuses one

When Heavenly Stewards bow in remembrance

Welcoming an out of place solstice

It was

What was this again?

That made this of worth?

Gone now home

We see no more

Till harvest moon comes

Till harvest moon comes

Reaper

Reaper lay waste the fields

Mice scurry about

Hawks, gazing eye

Ever knowing

With the Harvest

Comes the beasts to feast

Even mice know how to weep

Talons, talons delivering fear

Remember she whispered

Sing me a melody weird

Slap thy face clean

Crumbs fall to the floor

Mice cometh to the feast

Upon my broken soul

A Little Dab'll Do Ya!

Nothing's hard

Is it hard?

All of it

Hard on an individual being

Watching those two

Or one

As is the case with me

One or two for you?

One for me

Twas beyond enough

Oh, what a lover

Power encompassed

Image of cool

Eyes set to infinity

While living mortality

Oh, you

Peering, through the hour glass

There goes the sand

Building a mountain

From the Fall

Safe, until turned upside down

Growing old

Weak in frailty

Not being able

At one moment

Minuscule

Beholding everything

Wanting time back

Oh, please

What I'm viewing

Unbearable

This heart, breaking

The strongest person you'd know

Ever known

Who held you close

Loved you most

Even in all the fuck ups

From stupidity of youth

Still was there, with a smile and a cup of Joe

Here you go, kid!

Lost within a visionary past

Where is your hand?

There is nothing to hold

Now, as the clock arms swings ahead

Strength faded

Away it went

Strangest cruelty

Never

I don't understand

This feeble mind just cannot grasp

Teardrops not healing

Life sure is a bag of dicks

She was a dreamer

I know where I get it

She was exuberant

Courageous

When men weren't destroying her soul

Oh, mom

How I miss

That younger you

Full of life

Vibrant

Adventurous

Everything

God only knows what I'd be without you.

When you would sing me this

All the love in the whole of my world

Was in those eyes

Remnants of a torn and tattered memory

I'll just label it

Precious

While I carry on with life

I'm tryin to write

Doc Wonder, The Bastard, he's screwin with my keyboard

I walked away and gave up writing

Notes Don't State

There is Something Wrong with the Notes

He was an "ARTIST"

Making fancies

Using colored ink upon white things

Golden, whatever graffiti he laid

He would tell you so

"It's golden, as if touched by Apollo himself"

Sprayed from his lips

We just call that spittle kid

Obviously, the greatest there ever was

One, could just taste the arrogance

It was seeping testosterone

Spermies, rained all day

Salty white

Kinda off

Odd really

Who talks about this stuff?

How did this get?

This shit is really in the notes...wtf

Natural speaking my ass

"ARTIST"

The golden chosen one

His anus, housed the shit that didn't stink

Because he was an "ARTIST" of the highest rank

I got nothing, it's here in the notes!

Would tell you all day about his greatness

He could have any broad on the street

Typically, though, they would rest at his feet

Groveling for…meats?

That shit can't be right, let me double check the notes!

"Stripper # 48 stated: He has little cock, she was actually screaming it down the block"

"Stripper # 6 stated and I quote: "She couldn't even feel a thing and she's only 19" I'm a little lost as to what that means"

"Stripper # 24 Said she was going to cut it off if she could find it!"

Yikes, these broads are vicious.

Maybe I shouldn't say stripper?

Is Exotic Dancer more PC?

Doesn't appear anyone was groveling for meats.

"ARTIST" must have misinformed me

Damn this note taking, must have been high

A batch of tomfoolery

Mainly, strippers that got paid

Shit, Exotic dancers is so inconvenient

Always, always did the "ARTIST" ride

That Harley's Davidson's

It was super-duper charged

Pulling up to the Artistic shop

It was rev, rev, wanting to blow a window out

Always too cool for helmets

In the fashion army now

C'mon he's an "ARTIST" you people

Oakley sunglasses

Nothing less than two Franklins and change

Name brand Harley Davidson MotorsKooter jacket

It was stamped

Signed by Harley himself

Nice of his mother to pick it out

Thanks momma he would say

In the room

Where the "ARTIST" performs Artistry

Is absolute......filth

Roaches, fucking roaches

Used for placeholders with sticks

It didn't matter, he loved that shit

Just sat there chuckling

Even, if some health inspector was on their way

Could do this from a bedroom he would state

Even, with all this, extended confidence

The line was still out the door

Booked six month's out

Like some Boss

Arting the nudes is what he liked best

"ARTIST" didn't enjoy his Roomies

He wasn't about fair trade

On an off meds day, things became insane

Cigarette butts and business cards

Strewn all over the back room

In the bathroom

He made a Moana Lisa from his shit

It deserved a clear coat

"ARTIST" lost his mind over vacuuming

Wanted to choke people out

Mainly his Roomies

He's had enough

Treated like he's a Twelver

This shit ain't no grade school

An expert on being silent

Loved dishing out the cold shoulder

Giving those dirty looks

Except when Headstone was played

He'd weep like a little bitch

Moaning, bringing sound to a deaf ear

No "ARTIST" didn't care

Wasn't going to listen to that shit

He gave that band nothing but thumbs down

On occasion, like once or twice a week

When things would go wrong with the strippers

Fuck those exotic dancers

They'd express about his small cock

In the studio, down the block

Telling all the strangers

How the "ARTIST" has a little one

This transpired, more often, than not!

"ARTIST" always liked to flaunt

Telling the Roomies what they did wrong

Gosh damn expert in everything

Especially, when it came to choking people out

A small-town celebrity

This side of nowhere

Big shot in the realm of artistry

One day

When the meds were no more

A flashback to Nam often occurred

What the... this joker was never in Nam!
He wasn't even wet in his mother crotch
When Nam took place
These notes are filled with buffoonery

"ARTIST" was gone
Roomies threw a party
Did some remodeling
The place went wild
Long gone the days of pain
Cigarette butts and business cards
No longer Scatter the floor
Farewell, those days
When screaming strippers
Demanded to get paid
Business for the artistry with colored ink
On a more even keel
The ship seemed to sail

Where did "ARTIST" go?
The notes don't say
We can only guess

Perhaps, he found a new spot
With a new host to suck the juice from
One of those places
Where unicorns grow from his magical shit

The notes state

Roomies recently sent a care package
Remnants of cigarette butts and business cards
With a card that read

Thanks for not choking us out.
Best of luck with your new endeavor
It's great having you gone
Peace out suck a cock!

They Found Him Naked
With flesh neatly peeled.

Mothers Dish

Banging away

For days and days

This damn pitchfork

Discovering hope in the ground

Sweat, turnin eyes red

Up it goes

Down it comes

Day in

Day out

My mom

Remember

Mom

Stands in my bedroom

"Don't you ever be ashamed of yourself! You understand me Gocni?"

Don't you be ashamed

It echo's in my brain

Living life, on the downside of squalor

Don't be ashamed

At the feet of a magazine

Worshiping the image

Of what I'll never be

Freedom can be taken away

Treated as a privilege

Now, it's not a right

Don't be ashamed

Running some hot times

Inside my veins

Ride the bitch fast

Motherfuckers, I'm invincible

Hey man, everyone crashes

Go, go, go

So is the show

Don't be ashamed

What the hell does it even mean?

My mom's, always an endless question

Did she mean

The speculation in the brain

As dyslexia queries random shit

My mom would sit me down

Look at me

Study my being

All square in the eye

"Don't you rely on me for answers Gocni! Come to your own conclusion!"

But I'm only eight

Just a tilted blank stare

Like as if, don't even ask

I came to many conclusions

They were so wrong

That's cool

I conclude, my mom's insane

That's true

Side note:

Did you know

You can eat frozen Cool Whip!

I never came to that conclusion

Until about a year ago

Mom, lied to me!

Lied for a very long time...ridiculous

My mom would get drunk

She liked gin straight from the bottle

Skip the glass

Watched her myself, drink dudes under the table

Those men of ill repute

She would sit me down

Tears running

Blue Mascara painting beautiful a face

"You treat a woman good! You hear me Gocni?"

But mom, it's three AM

I've already concluded, you are crazy

This drunken stupor, just proves it a reality

But I'll never be ashamed mom

I'll never be ashamed

I'll treat women

The opposite of how you've been...treated!

Because you make shitty choices

I conclude

I never respected myself all that much

We forgot to have that sit-down

Life, just blew away on you

It's alright

Finally got the conclusion

In my quest to treat women as you instructed

I forgot to treat myself good

Ending up like you, mom

But I'm not ashamed

I was wrong in listening, my simple conclusion

I just did what you requested

The rest was up to my own conclusion

Now here we are

Thanks for the trust and free will mom.

Enough of the bullshit

You did great

IT RATTLES THE BRAIN

WHILE THE CRUSTY VAGINA

WHIMPERS AND COMPLAINS

PLEASE, PASS ME ANOTHER JOINT

THE GREEN DEVIL WILL DELIVER

OR IS THIS HELL?

Did you know, that women are thee most beautiful creatures to ever slither from the slime of evolution?

Who knew!

Desensitize Society

Listen to the melody

Green-hair, dancing, naked in the street

Where are the fucking parents?

Cooking chicken nuggets

Billions, inside the noise

Women, all looking the same

Man's worth, in a dic pic

Sex, selling for prime rib

Braggin, about advancements

Monkey, scratching his siliconized nut sack

Wondering in the clouds

"Advanced!"

Humanity

Mankind, sexist!

Politically correct my ass

We must worship felinity

Sold like a product

Hello Kitties

This fool

Locked in a church pew

Eyes taped open

Over the sheep

Priest with a loaded gun

Spraying his version of holiness

Calling it, his anointing

Yes, father, give us more

Leading to a slit throat

Still murdering for dirt

Hankering, for immortality

Take another pill bitch

Ending face down

The sign states in a ditch

"Do Not Disturb"

Energy dumped into darkness

Monetary gains

Death sells better than cocaine

Self-medicate

Future, nah fuck it!

Inject heroin

Downside of Middle Class

Now the poor

Former poor dead in the dirt

Live on their corpses

In the land of Can't Make It

Crack house replacing the church

Life on the doomsday express

Corporate slavery, slaves

Taking a turn in the bathroom

Last stall

Good and Plenty

Hit the pit

Coping

Zombies, walking the halls

No future

Blueprint flushed with the shit

Those living the streets

Viewing them as worms

Maggots, slithering along

One paycheck from Fuck Ville

That is all

One paycheck

From total hell

Contracts

Zero benefits

Fucked in the ass by a dildo

Labeled

"Healthcare"

They called it reform

Relying on Government

Just step in line

Got the popcorn? Check!

Picture show about to start

Feature film

A Greater Demise

Where are the fucking fuckity parents?

Kid screams for mommy

Tears, flooding off innocent's face

Mommy

Lost, she's inside the needle

Resting on the floor

At the local grocery store

Little one doesn't know how to save

Racing veins

Into euphoric Heaven

Lights out as the chicken nuggets burn

All eyes, looking for savior

Church doors closed

Another crack house emerged

Super man's a syringe

Tweeker's "blowing" Paul to pay Peter

Euthanize the world

Masses in a daze

Another soul, imprisoned in a small device

People divided, clashing crazies

War with each other

Over another politician

Politicians laugh

Injustice, growin, like weeds

Little Charlotte, little Charlotte

Raised by television

Parents!

As the house burns

Where in the fuck, are the parents?

Media going ape shit

Ratings, this shit brings in, ratings

Where are the fucking parents?

Little Charlotte

Burnt alive

Travesty of epic proportions

Questions start to roll

How does this happen?

Where is, this country going?

Oh, my God, prayers!

Social interaction

Tossing rocks...seeking to kill

Pack of rabid dogs

Unleashing dialect fitting for rats

Kings and Queens

Ruling the sewers of psychology

Voices, experts, every one of them

Dutch Uncles, the whole lot

Blonde bimbo playing journalist

Acting for a golden globe

Making millions

Selling propaganda

Blaming the parents

Not seeing the bigger picture

Wasn't part of the script

She's not that intelligent

Not paid to think, just smile and speak

Insects can't handle truth

Another Fox inside CNN spread wide

Moles don't know better

Condition them first

Working for less

Barely makin rent

In a rut of hopelessness

Starving people turn into a mob

Rip things down

Burn the town

Media calling for calm

Police informed

Gunning to kill all

Forget the protect and serving

This is the business of murder

Population control

It's only forty-five million or so

War zone in the neighborhood

Two broke fucks deciding to screw

Nine months later

Sliding out a little piss & shits

Screw it

Let's create a litter

Tossed into the pile

Hey there, Trevon

Born to a couple of losers off Skid Row

On the shit side, next to the landfill

Every part of life

Now, against him

Skin Color

Fighting the temptations of the curb

That get dropped on the street corner

Except this isn't the Sunday paper

Lines amass for another ride

Escape from hell in the good old US of Ass

Won't be seeing Snake B to save them

Trevon was a good kid

He loved going to school

Was a great footballer

Futile, attempting, laying in a pool of his blood

Media scum, projecting it as another sucker dead

He shouldn't have run

Police are innocent on this

He probably had a gun, at least, allegedly

Where are the fucking parents?

Strung out while working at a burger joint

Shooting up in a bush

Surviving on minimum wage

Fuck it all the same

The jobs they used to have got shipped away

Need to be competitive, so stated the CEO

After receiving

That two-hundred-million-dollar check

Manufactured for cheap

Shits still priced as if it's made by the Corporation

Slave of the U.S.

Just keep the lights on

On the downward slide

Where are the fucking parents?

Police, gun down that Green Hair, dancing naked

Bullets, cheaper than paper

Parents strung out

Children left screaming

Chicken nuggets...

Where are the parents?

While the world is burning

His body rested

Half on the side walk

Half on the street

His one eye closed

The other faced heaven

The heat made him bloated

All the human ants kept on truckin

Not one stopped to notice

He was just another worthless human

Farewell Tuna

Another story, another telling

Another cranking the reels in my head

Making time back track

Skipping towards day's past lived

When things were so simple...simply simplified

Darkness no ground

While in the light of your mother

Her tragedies many, oh, so many

Yet, hidden from innocent's sight

Resting down

Upon soft meadows

Moment of beauty

Tossed to the shadow

There, consider me

Vision this story

Vivid in one, single, feeling!

Color of love

Embracing tight

Remember, remember that feeling

Breath in thy flesh

Every sound you lived in

Rhythmic loving heart beats

How those strong hands

Held you close

Understand it's all but gone

Just captured in the mind

On some shitty eight-millimeter film

Worn thin

Stretching apart

Only sections now

Playing without sound

Resting in rot

Conversing with empty boxes

Everything

That made the show

No More

No more of everything

Boxes of emptiness running tears

Farewell Tuna, farewell

Away goes the sailboat

Waving beyond the forcefield

Adrift

Floating into the mystifying darkness

Upon the white curtain

Opening

Lost within

White is everything

Glowing bright

Those before

Those after

One single moment, all arrive

Be not deceived

It is nothing more than a planetary rotation

What rests beyond

Pure

This was the description

Jotted it down

Needed to know before it was gone

How can this be?

I will never be the same

Former old

Wide eyed

My conscious did perceive

Great beyond some mystery

Beauty, a momentary thing

Now, just lost in this maze

What was removed

Should have stayed

It was a winters day

The car pulled up

I was just a youngster

Remembering the look

Her time of happiness

Love walked with them

They played in the snow

I wanted to run to them

Was locked indoors

Twas their moment of bliss

What happened past this

Doesn't matter

Another American shipwreck

This moment, this moment!

Mattered this moment

When two are one in the embrace of love

Seeing love

Feeling love

Sacrificing love

Flaming love

Understanding that it's tough

Living without...love

This is my last memory

Of family

They come

When they see you

Going for something

Their only goal

To tear you down

Fuck them

Losers are all around

Journal entry: Who cares!

Dancing with a fighting chance

Or perhaps

For a fighting chance, was I dancing

Maybe, that is more accurate

What's your thoughts?

Don't look behind you

I'm right here in front of you

On the paper

It's OK, you can answer

I promise, it won't make you crazy

Hmm the silent type

Why you so afraid?

Don't make assumptions

Is that what you're stating?

Don't back step it

That shit

Etched upon a face

That unique shifting

Furrowing the brows, just a small bit!

Your eyes, tell the story

Sullen suspense

Ha-ha, I can't see you

Let's step away from crazy...Home James

It's been awhile

I was being selfish

Doing arts and craps

It was a long side dead for me

It's such an excitement

Full throttled, inverted

Nuts rush to the head

Creating the world…Beautifully nuked

Contemplated all day

What I would write

Free should be shit

Can't say it wouldn't be…justified

That's just not my style

Each time, I pour out this soul of mine

It must be above

Failure is not an option

When reading, another's work

Perceiving them better than me

Pushing harder

This reward is not for monetary gain

Nor petty fame

Something personal

Me, arrogant!

Did you hear the crowd laugh?

Damn right, I'm arrogant

Truest words

No one else will blow your horn

The lions eat

Wolves roam free

Tigers happily hunt man

Feast upon me

I will be something beautiful

Put me in my place, taught me, educated me, left me for dead in the outskirts of hell

MR. Hot Dogger

I was walking down Thirty-First street

This is an inspired story

I did walk along this street

What I'm about to tell you

Happened.

Just the names have been changed

Protecting the guilty

Fuck'em, that's why!

It was a standard winter's eve

Yeah, that white shit was all over the ground

My breath was thick

It was that fucking cold

It's two AM

Bar closing

Out pour the drunkards

Loud bullshit

Public intoxication

Where is the police?

Roaming free

Savaged pack of criminals

Dude wheels up his hot dog stand

Time to feed the inebriated ones

Fiver's where flying

Fat stacks growing

Big six inchers going down holes

It was laughter and peace

Till the cops showed up

It wasn't what you'd expect

Waiting for the paddy wagon to arrive

Now, any minute

Nope the cops

Those vicious vipers of law enforcement

Harassing Mr. Hot Dogger

He's impacting drunken disorderliness

Sobering people up

Making a profit for himself

There went the Icers Christmas bonus

Dear Icers

No more DUI's

Revenue, after hours flushed away

Mr. Hot Dogger dude

Delivering an argumentative fight

Something about refusing to pay

Did that officer just state?

Mr. Hot Dogger owed them a premium?

That shit, they called resisting

It's a threesome on the ground

Oh, dear me

Mr. Hot Dogger just bit that officer in the cheek

Some call that foreplay

Here come the haymakers

Oh hell, A left, A right, another left

Followed by the right

Head shifting back and forth

The look on that officer's face

Pleasurable orgasm

Shit, there just went Mr. Hot Dogger's eye

Insanity of laughter

A bottle of mustard

You know, the yellow ones

Didn't realize it would fit in the mouth like that

Not the boot, shit, don't do it

Smashing yellow mustard like a can

Mother fucker wants Hot Dogger dead

Two officers, destroying one hot dog stand

The till, AKA cash register, busted wide open

Odd, that all that money would simply, disappear!

Must have called that "evidence"

Now, tucked away in some fictional cage

Mr. Hot Dogger a bleeding carcass

With a smashed yellow bottle in his cocksucker

Half slung over into the road

Wouldn't you know

That not even an ambulance was called

Drunken slurs of speech

"Fuck the police" and something or other

Language of the average Joes

With Janes at their side

Other police show up

It's a hit squad

Business as usual

Time to make arrests

Quit resisting us

Arrests

Get the revenue up

Low and behold

Wouldn't you know

That tough fucker

Mr. Hot Dogger

Starts to arise like some modern-day Jesus Christ

That doesn't look very safe

Just stay down Mr. Hot Dogger

For Christ sake

Just stay down Mr. Hot Dogger

He just stumbles about

Like a ten-month-old trying to walk

It was a second that felt forever

His face just turned slowly

They just came out of nowhere

Two head lights

Traveling at a high velocity

There is no Kris Kringle in this tale

SORRY!

Rudolph, that poor bastard

All but hot sticks in someone's freezer

Fuck a Vegan!

It was that old up and over routine

The sound

Skull cracking a windshield

Flips and flips high into the air

My god, the exhale

Like someone

Ignited dynamite under Mr. Hot Dogger's ass

Squealing tires followed of course

By a large crash

Gravity can be such an enemy

Sending Hot Dogger crashing

All we saw

Raining ruby red with hot dogs

Don't forget the mustard

It was simply a bright yellow

The police look at each other

It was an amused disbelief

Who is going to do this paperwork?

Write it up

Just another drunk that stumbled about

Night walking on the Thirty-First

Oh, my god

You need therapy

Crazy anti-social derelict

I smoke to that

Toast you with this red stuff

Wine that is...maybe

Oh, the shit I've seen

The shit I've done

Lip's Pickled Eggs

Intro:

Good evening, good morning

Good who gives a "_ _ _ _"

You're reading the words from Gocni

Some just call me G

Others, Mr. Schindler

Please, just call me Gocni

In the next few minutes

We're going to go on a little road trip

Kids all strapped in the booster seats!

Together, it will be…something

Traveling, upon a distant dimension

Transcending into the world of fuckery

Turn off the lights

Sit your ass down

Drop a load in the shitter

Let the spirit guide

Make it, intimate!

Ignite

Inhale…deeper…deeper

Let it all out…that's it

Until your eyes pop

Inhale...deeper...deeper...deeper

Deeper...deep

Feel, the body start to get light

Exhale...slowly

Soothe yourself

Start to move, get up quickly

Strut firmly

Run the circle of time

Let what's written

This shit you're reading

Allow this, to be your open channel...opening

Allow the white spirit to enter in

That morning star is what they call it

Don't focus on the fear, care not

Allow the arms of many

Tearing into your flesh

This will all play out for the best

The tin hat folks will be up in arms

Conspiracy nuts creaming their pants

They got their picks and sticks

Coming to hang your ass

Worry not

Inhale

Give it zero...fucks

Exhale

Let your spirit be carried away

Bring forth the wings of change

Riding hard...fast

Repeat the steps

Pleasure requires steady air

Thrusting

IT takes hold

Skin ain't no water

Moist

Let out the moan

Skies bleed red

Horizon, a new shade of deep maroon

Innocent, those eyes exposed

Currently, a horror show

Carried you

Purposely villainy

Going zero to no place

Flip this story

Where does one go Lip?

Let's talk about

Lip's Pickled Eggs

He was a good boy

Living life

A brother's slave

Lip was a drinker

Had no care

It was a beer with pickled eggs

He consumed the same thing every day

Never said much

The joint was somewhat empty

Just not this day

Perhaps it was a case of

Waking on the wrong side of a tomb

Maybe, he got shit canned

This was the 1980's after all

Mill rat walks on in

Half drunken from the tavern down the hill

Coming in to order some more liquid filler

Lip doesn't pay a mind

He takes a bite

Juicy those pickled eggs

Mill Rat had an issue with the smell

Got into it with Lip

He was eating the egg

Ignoring a verbal assault

Just enjoying the fine pickling

Don't remember

Can't seem to recall

When he switched the egg in his hand

Mill Rat...Mill Rat...just didn't think

He had the ape-beast inside

Opened the cage

Monster on the loose

Some think quicker with their dick size

All just perspective

Fist went with the quickness

The brain thought

Shit this is the end

Blasting that stench,

Right out the corner pocket of Lips head

What's reality in a few seconds

Lightning cracks

Mill Rat throat punched

Lip's hand a speed of light

Mill Rat sat there for a few ticks of the clock

Before turning blue

Falling like an X-Mas spruce

Grasping while crashing

Those eyes full of panic

Curiosity, found me curious

Is his life...reflecting

I laughed

Breath mother fucker...breath deeper

Only thing that reminded me of AA

Lip, didn't pay any mind

Just salted another egg

Opened his mouth

Teeth sinking into white

Jaw moving, he was off to chewing

Pleasure written upon his face

Zero effects of what punched the clock

Bar Keep speed dials

Nine-One-One

"What's your emergency?"

She just blurts out something about someone

Didn't really matter

In walks the oddest of oddities

High Heels dressed in Red

Looking down upon an expiring Mill Rat

She bends over the top of him

Me, oh my, what an ass shoved into the air

Going on about needing a pen

Wanting a knife

Her breast size

Would indicate she's truly a Registered Nurse

Was that sexist?

It's a slice of this

A stab of that

Mill Rat's breathing air

It's a miracle

Police arrive

Ambulance hurries off

Bye, bye, Mill Rat, good luck

Lip, acting in self-defense

He's allowed to finish eating those eggs

High Heels

Wasn't even noticed by the guy

Even though, it's all she talked about

Eggs and beer

More beer

Years would go forward

Story of a hallmark moment at the bar

Lip, confided one day with the Bar Keep

It was just a bad day

Buried his mother prior

Guess, she always made him pickled eggs

Lip, simply trying to enjoy a lasting memory

He paid for Mill Rats medical bills

Wasn't required for him to do it

Just how stand up, Lip really is

High Heels and Mill Rat

Hooked up as to be expected

Had a slew of kids

We called them Hellions

Devils of the neighborhood

Modern version of a little house in poor town

As for me

I'm still kicking it here

Livin inside this war zone

Igniting my lighter

Hitting the green

Inhale, Deeper...deeper...deeper

        E-X-H-A-L-E

Ripped out of this brain

A Ball Crosses the Street

What is that love?

Sitting there, around midnight

Strutting the streets

High heels, long legs, mmm sexy

Stockings, thigh high

Enough to make wolves howl

Skirt bouncing with each strut

Cars parked in a line

Each window, a dame

Ass up; breasts out!

Another quick forty

Hole in the head

Blue whites

Strobe light effect

Two in the back of a car

Once rubbin fuzz

Now, curse words and tears

Officers loud laughter

Jail sentence and a fine

Divorce court, states the homeless... psychic?

A ball crosses the street

Just a kid

An ordinary amongst the universe

In a world where skin color doesn't mean shit

Dark in tone

In some out of world neighborhood

Just a shortcut

Heading home

Minding his own

Up rolls the Five-O

This ain't no TV show

Bubbles roll past

A sense of relief

PHEW!

No sir, these sausage links

Pull over few drives down

Out they waddle

Yogi and Boo-Boo bouncing

Straight outta baskets

Hurricane straight at the kid

Stopping him for, nothing!

Laying down the questions

Say he's……resisting!

Pulling out the guns

Taser costing ten bucks to charge

A bullet, seventy-nine cents

Humanistic conversation

Apparently useless with apes

Mow him down for what again?

Hole in the head

A mother serving food

Barely paying the bills

Watches the horror on the evening news

Don't stroll this world

Tread not certain territories

Government wants to execute the broke

Bust out a war on poverty

Plenty gonna die

Each and every time!

A ball crosses the street

She's a golden star

Real natural

All State Champion

Wrestling boys, men

Didn't mean shit

She grew up tough

Daddy was a drunk

Mommy a ragdoll

Depression filled her tank

Self-worth flushed down the drain

This fighting

Beating the male

Keeping her alive

The pain always there

Stabbing in those girly ears

Smoke the pipe

It removes all the emotion

Life starts to unravel

Teeth hit the floor

Championships a dream ages ago

The reaper scratching the window

Counting down to dinner

Just remember

She's a fighter

This turn for the worst

Just a blip on the map

Time to overcome the odds

Beat the addiction

Crawl back to the top

Achieving goals

Though, ha-ha that never happened

Discovered a ghost, behind the dumpster

On the corner

Fourth and Blues

Down from Dr. Doom's

Maybe you heard it on the news?

Probably not

Star Athlete, dead from an overdose

A ball crosses the street

He's a student

Learning the great book

Seeking the wealth

Attending the markets

Purchasing a grow tall

Like a big slurp

Calculating the fall

Buying a loss

Another part of the system

Living large

Betting against the odds

Top of the world yo

Traveling abroad

Social media posting

Cruising in a new Ferrari

Look at this kid go

Line up the coke

Buy a super model

Down it comes

Top of the building

Thousands in soft hands

Looking upon the ants

One step off

Freeride

Splat onto the car

Hole in the head

In the chaos

Let those gather the funds

Ignoring the life lost

A ball crosses the street

Two in love

It's a journey

They give everything they got

Maintaining respect

Front of the church

Preacher paints eternity

Till death

Nothing other

It's the typical scene

Careers

Home having kids

Watching life disappear

Together

No quit

The struggles are there

Making it

Never easy

Life in the fast lane

Down the road, kids, long gone

It's two old fools

Loving each other

The way it should be

That's how it's sold in a platinum book store

Each to their own

Hope you make it

Life is tuff

Nothing comes free

Fuck what the millennials think

The real world has its own rules

Streets don't give a rip

Shit that comes easy!

Doesn't last

Love is a job

Coming from both sides

Working sun up to sun down

Peace Out!

In nothing is what?   *EVERYTHING!*

Drinking My Pain Away

Listening to you sing

That poetry makes me weep

Beauty shines in a soft voice

Angels fly nigh from those luscious lips

Fuck drunk in your song

Sing, sing, sing melodies of lyrical sex

Rape my innocence

Allow me this dance

In the rain, of your salty sweat

Look down upon me

You Rockstar goddess

With deep rich eyes

Peer into this porn

Sing, sing, sing, penetrate my madness

Reach down, pull my hair

Spit in my face

Call me, lover fucker

Make this shit wild

Place that stiletto upon my forehead

ited

Christ

ground

Bouncing my head like a ball

Wonder the majestic

Sing, Sing, sing vulgarities of love

Scream the world bright

Nothing compares to you in white

Loving the flowing light brown highlights

Shimmering in the STAR light

Kiss, kiss

Romance this broken soul

Make me dream the cream

Sing, Sing, Sing, ragtime my flesh

Tear this shirt off

Feel a six pack

Wink at me

Lifted hand blowing me away

Putting holes in thy chest

Strut that ass

Please don't wander away

I'm owned

Sing, Sing, sing to your slave

Bring me close

Erotic your voice in my ear

"You look hot baby"

Take my beer

Dump it over my head

Baptized in it

Drunken courage is the best

Treat me badly in your Dark Paradise

Sing, Sing, sing to this million less dollar clown

Show me queen

Watch this dog grovel

To feel those kinky feet

Divinity in my presence

Revive this dead fool

Another mutt

Alive again

Sing, Sing, Sing
Sing, Sing, Sing

Make this being lose his shit
Romance a corrupting spirit
Let our colors collide
Blow my twilight
Make me your bad boy
Let me show you man
You, celestial tellurian
Watch me lead you in strong arms
Through the dark door

Sing, Sing, Sing, what you need me to be
Holding you tight
Fight me, with your, mighty might
Dig those claws inside this skin
Demand me
Command this character
Build you a rocket ship
Drive you to Mars
Around this vastness of night

Beamed to the great beyond

Sing, Sing, Sing, into this moment

Bring in that great philosophy

Cure this diseased flesh

Allow this dream to never end

Love lost in your song

Time, to end, another concert

Lights go dim

That last look

Every time my cry lids come crashing closed

You are

Stained within these pain lenses

Sing to this broken heart

Sing, sing to me one last time

Goodbye as you ascend

Don't know how

This chest beats

For your tone

Its lights out

Farewell goddess

Farewell Elizabeth

Remember this dumpster

Flying down the ONE

With love

She had the voice of an angel

The soul of the Devil

Her touch

Frozen

She was just another corpse

Inside my mental freezer

Typical the Standards

Was just your ordinary Sunday Morn

Most likely, people stepping into a church

Sitting in a pew

Singing a melody that no one would ever hear

Who gives a rip

Not one in the sky

Birds, only look down for food

Listing to the Preacher spread the news

Crucible that death crucifix

Stealing from the pockets

Sticking cock in a tight ass

Shove it

Sinners, in the heat of it all

This wasn't an average normal Sunday

Not at all

The time

Eleven AM

Note it down

Eleven O One

To be a fact

Nineteen Eighty-Seven Something

It wasn't a day for singing praises

To the man in the clouds

I, just a kid

Playing my NES

Mike Tyson's Punch Out

Mike was my hero

A true champion

Taking no shit

Just a fool's face at the end of his fists

Ruled with a solid Peek-a-Boo

I was lined up to beat this Video Game

Fighting for my existence

Against that Mr. Sandman

He was trying to deliver

A signature

Dreamland Express

Though, this wasn't a Denver song

Screw that clown

Typical, for this average Sunday Morn

Wanting to climb into that ring

To dethrone my hero

Mike Tyson God of the Ring

Normally, when the guests come

It's a knock on the door

No, on this typical Sunday

More like a metal rod knocking it to the ground

I was startled

It was loud

My eyes, lost to the sounds

The weed of fear

Choking me

Holding me down

Little Mac was sent to the mat

SCREAMS to be GLORIOUS

"DEA, you MOTHER FUCKER"

"Get on the fucking ground"

The disguised human war thugs

With high-powered firearms

White was the DEA logo

Painted upon bullet proof vests.

I, the only one in the house

The bar beneath my face

Face of youth

Smashed eloquently into Shag

The noise vibrated in the floor

It was a soft sound

Quieter than usual

Living above a tavern

Always loud

Not on this average Sunday fun day

The tune echoing to this day

Cocaine by E.C

It was quite fitting

The maniac DEA all crazed

Screaming in my face

"Is there anyone else upstairs"

No, was my teary-eyed whisper

Behold, the hidden stairs to the tavern below

Down they funneled

Like a whirlpool of shit

Floating, towards the great abyss

Demons, reclaiming what was lost

Blazing cannons was the vibrations

Innocence of hearing, heard the vile

Screaming women in a bull horn

Shouting men, going to war

Bang, bang, boom, bang, bang

Thud, thud

INSANE

Was it just the drums?

A new tune from the jukebox?

Red and white painted the scene

Thirteen, remember that sacred number

Thirteen of the hidden god

It was the number of kilos

The DEA would later count

Remember wandering down

The dead guy

Resting half on the pool table

Whiteness spread across the floor

The green felt

Turning a different shade from open veins

Make this shit PG

Call it blue

He was another Smurf

Leaking like a slushy

A man cuffed on the ground

He's crying now

The overtone

Seeking the three that fled

A woman screams

Shouting

"Get the fuck out of here!"

A voice I knew well

Though, it's lost in this timeless crisis

Does it matter now?

Eyes to be desensitized

Death and destruction

All around

Money for power

Drugs without tax

A government can't have this

"A mother screaming at the immortals"

Kid was the shout

"Christ"

Swept up with the greatest of ease

Big black strong arms

Carried back up the stairs

Sat down in front of the Television

His tone, gentle, yet mighty

Asking me rightly

"You play this kid?"

Head just shakes for yes

Handing me a controller

"Show me how!"

Little Mac getting back off the mat

Knocking the dust off

Time to start again

Going to knock Glass Joe to the ground

Time to capture the video crown

Take the hero down

Show the world how

All on your standard Sunday Morn

Me and this new pal

Fuck that preacher man

My friend, the immortal DEA man.

Sitting down with this humanistic rodent
Resting on the ground
Twelve-gauge life giver
It wasn't inside a church
Not the average type that is
Just another drug bar
Where life was made whole

Heaven
Amid a kingdom above
Hell
While the blood ran white below

Give them a six-figure number
The media to promote the ratings
For brains in a frying pan
Didn't mean dick
To beating the god of Mike Tyson
We had something wonderful
Mike Tyson's Punch Out
With a man, immortal in scope
Sitting on the floor
Average, this Sunday everyday event

Welcome to this new church

In the grail of an NES

Time to take down

Mike

SURVIVED

The difference

Between you and I

Jesus, Bring the Check

It was one of those last-minute decisions

Late at night, the drunkards calling time

Craving eggs and coffee,

Reality, just the marijuana talking to my brain

Who was bitching at my stomach.

Maybe, the other way around,

Not that it mattered!

Food is what was desired,

Food is the only reason,

For this moment,

In my current state of mental season.

Watching the human doppelganger experience,

Called entertainment.

Doing what Momma said was eavesdropping.

At the cafe, the other night

Got me one of those male waiters

Coffee black, no cream please

Eggs, sunny side up, like life

The conversations full of slurred zing

A young gal, looking up at a young man

Her left on his right

Love, their countenance, in this particular time

Across from me

Couple of fellas talking religion

One: Thinking it's nonsense

Other: Still on the fence

It was a cat and mouse event

My thought: shits only provable upon death

One: Stating a discord with Jesus Christ

Other: Mixed on opinion

The Waiter

Plate of eggs, coffee black

Can I get you anything else?

Just shaking my head

Man, that was fast

Shouting though, got my attention quick

One: Blaming every war on one man, one religion!

Other: Explaining the difference in times

A young gal looking up at a young man

Smiling and giggling

Heeding no cares but being loved

I'm Sitting here, poking the golden goodness

Spewing over white as I sip my coffee of nakedness

Shit's not very good

Same price as someone Amazon book

What did you expect for thirty-nine cents?

Fork for the civilized or I'd use my hand

Going in my mouth

One way or the other

With no give a damn's

The conversation getting lively

One: Heated on how Jesus Christ destroyed the lands

Other: No longer talking

Sad how his face was void of reasoning

Piece of egg in my hole

Down it goes

Hoping not to choke while listening to this joke

One: Exploring onto Hindu, Buddhist

So forth it goes, down the line

Screwing the alphabet right

Other: Interjects some form of logic

Without of course, knowledge

Another egg down the pipe

Into an empty acid filled dungeon

Heightened senses

Make it so much better

Coffee, like a fine wine,

So, it seemed, if that is even possible

Or it's the ganja making everything demented

Either way, who cares, it is excellent to eat

Whilst listening to a mundane conversation

Momma said eavesdropping wasn't polite

Never really cared what Momma said any 'Ol'ways

One: Proclaiming how everyone is brainwashed

Other: Attempting to state how religion helps save

Making fun of the glue holding it together

A partially successful society

It's on me to think,

Ponder

Oh, how so many, can't walk life alone

Great, keeping things chained, making it safe

Needing something at the end gate

One: Stating that it's just how he feels, how it is

Other: Giving an acceptance spiel

They should hug

They should kiss

Fuck it, just make out

Kick it the right way

I'll drop some Georges to see that shit

Oh, shit, wrong story

Forgotten this is a café

Not a stripper's dirty paradise.

Eggs gone, coffee empty

Where the hell is my waiter

Jesus bring the check

Piece of toast in my hand

Shit better not be gluten free

One and the Other leave the table

Didn't even leave a tip

Cheap pricks

Guess they missed that service

Compassion for those just getting along with it

A young gal, looking up at a young man

Their current love state

Paid no notice to any of this madness

Just lost in the moment together

My wish for them, that it never ends

I'm no religious fella

Vital though, to a functioning prison society

Not really one to disrespect

What someone else perceives as nonfiction

Even though

Occasionally it's good humor to rip

Like another Pinocchio

Not God, that name is reserved

For a woman of the night with legs up high

Wolves set lose in the bedroom

Partaking in fleshly things

Peter Pan is banging who?

Captain Hook!

You don't say, you don't say

From what I heard about Jesus

Love thy neighbor as self

Forgive your brother quick

Turn the other cheek

Help those in need

The other religions each taking consideration

Good and evil in the world of citizen Q

I give zero shits about religion

Following another human being

Who's attempting a shot at god's right hand

Just doesn't appeal to me

Leading others blindly down an ally at night

Kids shouldn't wonder down a dangerous path

Less you drink the Kool Aid off a psycho's lips

Only pondering the words from another

Who walked the earth

Seeking something higher than self

Forgetting material nonsense

Pointing out errors in the direst of times

Shit, I'm monologuing

Oh, here he comes, my personal Jesus

Finally, the check

Leaving the tip

Got some cheap asses to make up for

Tip's to make the chit

Our true religion, Dollar bills

He brought you a sandwich

Cafe all but a blur down the road.

Nighttime creatures roaming the streets

In the dark, purest humanity

Never smoke the crack, no, not ever!

I Remember America

Once, when I was younger

Though, not older

I remember this country

Marveled at its girth

Was once called America

Home of the who knows?

It was a place

Where they did things

Built wonders

Worked together

It was never perfect

Was just another illusion

Childish imagination

Propaganda of the youth's brain

Read this version of history

Creating the fairy tale

Though, the thought

Fragile to the whisper

Shattered

I'm older now

Though, I'm not ancient

I remember this country

Was once called America

A place where the disease of fear took precedence

Gave complacency to stupidity

Where the term "war" consumed the insane

Killing folks, worldwide

All for a media boost

WAR

On poverty, the homeless die

On Drugs, Prison's resemble cities

On countries, they lay in waste

Label it: A Digital COLOSSEUM

Spoon fed to the masses

Right up there with baby slop

Eagerly consumed

A poison injected into the brain

Give me war dear brother

Bang, bang, everyone's dead

I'm missing limbs

Brother is in a million pieces

I'm gazing into his eye

Dearest sister

Stitch us back together

Please make us whole

Wrap us in the flag

Send me to the grave

I'm happy the investor

Profited ten percent

"Pray with me"

States the conman

In a black robe

This modern version of Rome

Stir the emotion

Shout it on the corner

Sell it from the pulpit

Empty the Mental institutions

Insanity for the dogs

Watch them drop from the golden bridge

Please fall headfirst

Filling the cells

Obviously, cheaper, isn't it?

Smoke the lady

The vile escaper

Get a needed twenty to life

That will teach them

Cardboard mansions

Fulfill the gutter dream

Now we love that

Wealthy walk past

The sweet fragrance

What is that?

No dear, that's not roses

We call it shit mixed with piss

Want a sip?

I'm ancient now

Soon will be dead

Wanting to state

I remember this country

Was once called America the great

She really had the kicks

Don't really recall what made it

Themselves the people divided

Fighting for a sliver of dust

Pretending to elect fictional leaders

Trusting their loving government

Way beyond self

Losing faith in their own ability

She sure was amazing

I remember

America

I got nothing, not a thing...

Water Chestnuts

Treading the waters of doom

Swimming in my own chaos

Caught in the rapids of time

Hell's grip is upon me

Lost in the system

Sink or swim

Head just above water

Lamprey attaching to my limbs

Draining this humanistic juice box

Fight is fleeing the scene

Under goes the nose

Lungs trading water for air

This fish has lost its fins

Sinking to the bottom

That final explosion of the brain

Opening the doorway

Perceiving the hidden

Mystical DMT

The lights flicker

Annoying the beeping

Some sickening moaning

Groaning

Faint red clock flashing

Three AM

Just one of those very oddities

Oh, for Christ sake

It's just that old hag

Sitting in the corner

Trying to be scary

Bounce a size 11 off her skull

Bitch floats away screaming

Cries, echoing through the hall

An outspoken thought

"It gets out and it stays out!"

Back to peaceful

Shit stain old bag

Lost her way to the morgue

The problem has been resolved

Time to get back to the drowning.

She was a billion miles

From my back yard

Time slipped by

Our short eternity

Gone

Twas Justice

On another May Day

Life was blossoming

Inside a gentle being

Love birds singing

A Monarch landing upon a nose

Laughter filling a world

Creatures of innocence

Sitting on the side of a path

Massive those old souls

Mighty Oaks

Glorious Maples

Haughty Pines

Simple Ash

Bowing down

The great Apples

Releasing their flowers

The Unseen Spirit

Lining a gentle path

White petals upon the flesh of Paradise

The walk short

Life continually growing

Suddenly going row

Blue skies turning gray

Lightning striking those massive trees

Igniting in flames

The Unseen Spirit

Suddenly torn Evil

Clouds rolling as large spears

With Devilish faces

Laughter of scorn

Now filling the world

Life has changed

Though, still growing

Love birds, imprisoned in the flames

Songs to sing no longer

Least they had each other

While they perished

Precious the Monarch

Now captured in a Hawks claw

Apple trees once so loving

Withered to dust

Simple the path

Now a river of mud

Cold and wet

Numbing the gentle being

Dimming another light

Darkness bringing weary

A Sky weeping

Clear water, now shades of red

Forever a short walk

In pain comes life

Light screams through the faces of dread

Skies open wide

Wicked runs to hide

Love birds multiplied

Melodies with emotional release

Monarchs in the number of stars

Gentle to the touch

Sun birthing peace

Life is Born

Breathing mortality inside

Connecting spirit to flesh

Exhaling eternity

Beauty gone dead

Emptiness, filling the world with silence

Flaming Rocks

Blasting through the firmament

Like beasts

Burrowing deepest of holes

Cracking the whole of love in two

Love birds turned statues

Monarchs to star dust

A sky without form
Sun is no more

Trees

Mighty Oaks

Glorious Maples

Haughty Pines

Simple Ash

Leafless and dead

Prairies washed into a desert bed

Lost, the creatures of innocence

Skeletons in a wasteland

Nothingness

Destruction the only sight

A gentle being gazes

Left to endure this tragedy

The pulse of hope

Flat Lined

Injustice Twas

Wandering to understanding

Answers all around

Truth

None to be found

Just a flash of light

Imagery of the former

Massive the old souls

Mighty Oaks

Glorious Maples

Haughty Pines

Simple Ash

Love bird's music

Sweet to a deceased spirit

Precious those Monarch's

Soothing with whispers

Creatures of Innocence never ending

Unseen Spirit returning

Balance

Sun maintaining

Gentle being

Just a stone

Gazing a vast horizon

But Look

Behold

One green stem

Growing within the cracks

So, it goes

Life begins again

This Bit of Something

Was it just honey?

No, it was more than

SOMETHING

Had I laughed it off

It may not have felt like a dream

Time has gone

Fast, so fast

It's a light before the eyes

Why can't I stop this ride?

It's right there in the mind

That vision

Touchable, yet far, far away from thy arm

My life, a puff of smoke

Soon dissipated

You were reading something above

It was the story of

Something

The tale of a being
Bringing life into the world

Everything was beautiful

Planned and Perfected

Something

An appointment sent it to the abyss

The road was short

Yet went on forever

Life came in the pains

Took a breath, then left

Flew away on wings

Everything vanished

All that remained

Was stone cold flesh

I enjoy a small whisper over a loud voice
Also, I'm quite fond of Dunkin' Donuts coffee, its super good

Writing slipped my mind

Took a much-needed break

Negativity can kind of drain

Writing

When it's for pleasure

For Self, then writing is beneficial

Enjoyably fun

When attempting to appease some larger scope

Well, then, it all goes to wrong!

Nothing to really care about

You may be reading this

That's cool

Though, please understand, this writing

All of my writings, in fact, aren't necessarily for you

Some may state

"Going to give that Gocni a real Bollocking!"

"That's a real working of a shit sandwich Gocni."

I respect that

Enjoy the thought of it

Believing you to be real in an opinion

Dare I concern myself?

No, not in the least

Absolutely not!

Please, don't be insulted

I wasn't insulted by the fact you didn't like it

Just don't fucking care what you think.

Cause my writings aren't for you

I wrote them for me

Enjoyed it so much

That it puts a huge smile on my face

"Aint going to get rich doing it that way!"

Ahh, wealth, money, fame, fortune

That miniature castle

With a hundred rooms

Let me blow my top

Want me to write a character

Have him beaten down with fear?

Give him the no friend treatment

Against all odds

Only to overcome the fear

Find true love

And now

Everyone loves him

For a story

He triumphed and won

That is what the standard human

Requires in a story

Shall we then

Pull our pants down?

See who's got the bigger stock

Or would you rather wait till later?

No, it's not important

More on the lines of, who owns who

You see, the trouble we have

Is everyone, is an expert

Every book is cheaper than coffee

They're all here to voice their opinions

The whole of the world should stop

Get down on bended knee

"Time for a little ass kissing Steve"

While the five second King/Queen Proclaims

"Going to save the planet from this written Gocni."

Suddenly, everyone knows

What everyone else will like

Who blessed someone with this kind of power?

Who has the right to define what art is to another?

Can I please meet this deity?

Bullshit

I find Romance and Erotic stories

To be lame and boring.

Would I put on that pair of balls?

Making some statement

That say these stories aren't good!

That somehow, my word, is that of a God

Hell no, hell no I wouldn't

Who am I, but a singular digit?

The point I make is this

I'm not on American Idol

Or competing on some

Authors World reality show

I'm a person, who likes to write

Feelings are here, sometimes.

Nothing more

Not claiming to be great

Don't really care about that either

Really, not my place to state

Not into what you're reading

Then please just go

No harm, no foul

Just don't send me a nastygram

Proclaiming your version of worth

My worth, is more than anyone would know.

Peace Yo; Love you so!

Shit Writing

Not long ago

The conversation, debatable

Discussing stealing work

In regard to "work"

The terminology

A written story

Settled to paper

To be placed in a binding

It was over nothing

"You need to protect yourself"

Those cheaters of the night

Pinked in attire

Slithering along like a corrupted snail

Copy while pasting

Treating it, like their own

Laughable

"How is that funny"

Monkey, can write about playing with the ding-a-ling

Because this clown

Could write about taking a shit

Making it loverly

Or was it

Loverly making it

Don't think that matters

Laughter around the table

So, as it is

"Prove it"

Great

An axe, tossed between two feet

Going to be like that Viking's Queen

What's her name?

Lagertha, played by that bombshell

Katheryn, let me bite my fist, so hot--Winnick

I'm not only fan but a super stalker

Hmm, maybe that came off wrong. I'm into beautiful things!

Shit, I got side tracked

Well, maybe we'll start like this

There was this guy, walking down the hall

Nope, he was almost hobbling

Holding his legs together, tightly

More like some dance

Yeah, more like a skippin dance

He's discovered on the camera

Not that some guy watching it cares

He's only making nine dollars an hour

Basically, affording to live with the roaches

Funny, how the guy hired to protect the place

Makes the least!

This one video

Call it, an instant break through

Is going to make him some cash

Not filthy rich

Just a little extra spending money

He just doesn't know it yet

Don't say anything

Be quiet about it

The guy walking

No, wasn't walking

It was this

Legs crossed dance

Finally, he makes it to the bathroom

Oh, no!

Damn the luck

Out of order

Temporarily closed

Shit, what is one going to do?

Corrected

What is he going to do?

The Security Guard is full of curiosity

Filter

Alright a little zoom

Perfect

Yeah, no one is looking

Really, the mop bucket

Down with the pants

Fingernails, digging into plastic

Face towards the ceiling

Must be one of those liquid types

Another round, call it

Two

Damn near emptying the large intestines

That poor mop bucket

Looking around

What will one wipe with?

Didn't think of that

Bright idea

Right there above your head

Just reach up and grab it

Take the pants off

Hopping on one leg

Taking pants off while still wearing shoes

Always such a hassle

Oh, you think you know what's going to happen

Of course, you do

Of course, you do

That was intentional

The two, Of course 'you do's'

Let's rewind the tape

There is our hero

Dropping a load

Dancing down the hall

All backwards

Ten minutes' prior

Stop, hit play

A woman walks down the same hall

She's in a dress

Color is red

No, she doesn't have a picnic basket

Wrong story chums

There, she strolls down the hall

Into the woman's restroom

Never was it out of service

Women's are always open

Unfortunately, the camera doesn't work in there

But lucky for you, we have god mode

Time to get tuned in

Put the head set on

Little fuzzy, one moment

There that should be great

Three bathroom stalls

Middle stall occupied

"Are we looking through her eyes?"

I did say god mode, didn't I!

Looking at beautiful, in a mirror

"Prrrrrt!"

Oh, what was that?

She just let one rip

Fucking, not lady like at all!

Great to know we got sound

Walking to the last stall

Opening the door

Stepping inside

What happened to the sound?

Technical difficulties

Always an excuse

Sliding down the panties

No, you're supposed to use that paper over the seat

Hocking up the dress

Sitting down

Gross

Enduring more of the

"Prrrrrt!"

When the sound came back on

Then came the

"WHOOOOOF!"

Followed by a huge splashing

Did someone just set of a nuke in the ass?

No!

Are we sure?

No!

Reaching for some ass wipe

What was that?

Did you see it?

No!

Look again!

No!

Right there!

No!

A shiny thing

Red light

That's a phone set to record

The character next stall is a creeper

Time for some justice

Better wipe first

Up come the panties

Down with the dress

Out the door

Watching the floor

Oh, I'm so excited

Middle stall

Scrawny hand reaches down

Picking up the phone

That's it

Washing the hands first

Peering a blank mirror

What a great Five O'clock Shadow

Suddenly, the body turns fast

One high heel

Size thirteen

Turns into some judo kick

Blasting the middle stall door

Wide open

Perp

There he sits

Eye wide in terror

With a phone in his left hand

Dick in the right

One broad in a red dress violently reaching

Two massive hands

Gripping the jacket

Of a sick Masturbator

Ripping the character out of the stall

Phone slides across the floor

Muscular arms, such definition

Turning the character around

It's almost like a dance

Round and round

Swing your partner dosey doe

No!

One hand on the back

The other on the ass

Time to get 86'd out the door

Ramming the character's head into the door

It was only a few times

A door swings open

Character fighting

One man bouncing up and down

Trying to get his pants off

A lady in a red dress

"There is more of you!"

The man jumping up and down

Starts to turn

There is no understanding

Without hesitation

Tossing the Character out the door

Directly into the fella

Obviously trying to take his

Pants off

Both fall

Oh god, right over that mop bucket

Its water and shit all over the floor

That poor fella trying to get his pants off

Gets the worst of it

The Masturbator tries to flee

Slipping and falling

From the liquid shit

It's impossible for a foot to get a grip

That poor man

With his pants stuck on his shoe

Dripping full of shit

Head to toe

This beauty

Captured on record

Security is dispatched

Though, maintenance makes it first

Our friendly neighborhood Masturbator

Has escaped

Though, he did leave his phone

Evidence

That guy, who took a shit inside the mop bucket

He's a professor, who knew?

Ended up with some stomach bug

The lady in the Red Dress

She's a woman trapped in man's flesh

The Masturbator

At large to this day

The security guard

Twenty Million views later

Received a little payday

Could finally buy that wedding band

Nice down payment for the dream house

White picket feces and all!

All because something amazing happened

When someone had to drop a load

This shit never happened

It was made up in about a half an hour

More like, I just wrote it

You could call it fresh off the press

No planning

Just doing

Remember

If you come to sit at my table

Eating the food upon my plate

Take it all

Leave nothing to remain

For my kitchen is stocked daily

My gardens full

Nothing do I have in want

So, please

Take it all

Leave nothing to remain

RELIGION
Our only blue print
That everything will be alright
Possibly bullshit
But it is a good bullshit
That has a high sales volume

Hope

If I recall the word
With its inheritable worth
It's often described as a blue print
Guiding us to something more

Hope

Great this life line
No matter how far we go astray
Regardless of some perilous event
Leading one to a darkened pit

Hope

Least one should not lose sight of it
When growing up
Twas just a little fellow
My sperm donor took off
Now, my free-spirited mom
She was awesome in her youth
Always an open door
Give help to those who had none

Hope

It was then, that the four Cubans would come too live
Only one, spoke a lick of English
The three, simply Spanish
It was nice having them with us
For that time
The three, eventually left
Where they went
I have not a clue
Though, I do think of them from time to time
On the other hand
One remained
He spoke English

Was like a father figure to me
Though, it wasn't his duty
He was a bit of a brute
As, he wasn't that old at the time
Young twenties
Maybe twenty-one
I was probably more like a little brother
But shit, I was young and was looking

Hope

Nature has a programmed code
Boys need to learn from a man
They also need to learn from a mom
See, I already had that!
As time progressed
Twas when I be thirteen
He finally met someone
They moved away
Was hard seeing him go

Hope

That we would stay in touch
Everyone else always just left
He ended up having a couple kids
I got to know them well
Time moved along
As it always does
Life was in the fast lane
Speeding it away
I didn't see him as much
That is how the story went

Hope

He contacted me once
After I had a kid of my own
Told me he was proud of me
Happy that I changed my life around

Told me he believed in me
I can do anything
Never did I feel so

Hope

Sometime went along
His kids grew
The youngest still living at home
One of those phone calls
He died of a heart attack in the front yard
Just turned fifty years' old
My heart wept
At the funeral
I met his family
The remainder that fled Cuba
It was a lot of tall tales
Great the memories

Hope

Like the damn throttle is stuck
Time progressed
I was talking with his boy
On that Facebook
He was running the virtual mouth
We would call that typing
It brought humor
I knew the type of talk
He was a chip off the old block
Reminded him
His papa would be proud
The tune quickly changed
Indicating
A thank you
It was a worry he couldn't shake
Something he desperately needed to hear
Especially coming from me

Hope

One thing I knew for certain
Without any doubts
This kids father, loved him more, than life itself
Kindly, just added
No need to worry kid, worry isn't something that is needed
Your Papa loved you, it's the only thing you need to focus on.

Hope

Me being the closed door
Always that tougher exterior
It didn't dawn on me
What he was actually enduring
Hoping that he was doing it right
Not knowing what his Papa would be thinking
Hard, that must be
Not knowing
Life is riding the short bus
Just around the corner
Done!

For you Sir, thanks for being something you didn't have to be
Hope

The Expected reject of Expectation

It was an expectation

Always, some form of intent

The standard

That hopeful breaking point

I remember my first boss

He was fat

Wasn't doing the job to his

Well, now you know, don't you!

That graceful voice

Teeth, still housing tobacco

Stench of death upon the breath

In this face

Delivering a message

"Boy, if you don't make this mark, that's it, down to loser lane!"

That was it

All that it took

Didn't make the mark

Exceeding, that... expectation

That's good, right?

No, just wait for the day

When the new mark isn't obtained

Dear me, why?

It's always a game

Let us play, the better

No second rate

That boss of mine

Looked at me

From a different perspective

Dependable

Taught me how to drive a car

Special favors

All because of that, great expectation

Now, it wasn't always me

Others came to work

Only, three made the mark

What I was out of three

Doesn't matter

Who cares about the number!

It was just shoveling shit

Building muscular character

Eventually, I walked

Didn't matter

Needing, desiring, something else

Seeing his fat bald head

Rotting black teeth

That dragon breath

Those words

"Boy, you gonna go far if you keep to that work ethic."

The expectation set

Work

Never was I school bound

Too stupid

Some sort of remark from that guiding light

We called a school counselor

I too, gained an expectation

While I was expected to fail

School teachers

Guidance counselors

I give them the expectation

Of worthless human beings

CUNTS!

(disclaimer: I didn't call any woman this, I enjoy my life.)

I'm not sorry for my opinion

CUNTS!

What was delivered to me!

Here is

The mark of mediocrity

I lost a footing

That expectation, just couldn't be met

Not when there is no self-respect

I met the expectation

Self-destruction

I didn't disappoint in that area

No sir!

This too, needed a change

Attire, just wasn't in style

Worked some shitty jobs

A clown with no High School Diploma

That's the expectation

It was bottom dweller gigs

Who cares

I sure didn't

Fucking notion of assumption

Rebellious

Back to another expectation

Wanting that American dream scape

Meeting a young girl

Running into the unknown of marriage

BONDAGE

That father figure

Protecting his little princess

"Son, you want to marry my little girl you need to get that diploma."

There it is

Expectation

Which I complied with

Got me married

The real American dreamer

Next, would follow a whole slew of

Bigger, better, more expectations!

Expectation of time

Steady expectation of income

Another expectation of building a home

That birds nest

Preparing for those darlings

I expect you to be here

Not checked out

Expecting while in Expectation

The bar

Higher than life

Women set this bar

Do they subconsciously love to see their mate fail?

Gives them something to gripe to mother about

Then she too can scowl

Something that is most cherished

While playing the Betty Crocker

"Your Father told you not to marry that worthless boy."

Always some major fucking let down

Sir,

"Bloody Christ, what is it boy?"

Captain is drunk at the wheel, Sir!

"Cack-handed Plonker, Ahh Christ there is piss and Vomit everywhere!"

Sir!!

"What now boy?"

Look Sir

"Brace for impact chaps!"

"Best know how to swim"

"The ships going down"

Sir?

"Christ boy, what!"

"Sir, I can't swim…"

Another missed expectation

This expectation:

Will never make the mark

When your face down,

Breathing earth

Expectation to rise again

The Spiritual expectation

Finding the expected purpose

Living for an expecting being

Ruthless within impossibility

Someone is expecting death

Another is expecting life

Expecting a soul swap

Meanwhile, I'm still expecting my damn free lunch

It sure is a good kick in the nuts

When you finished your soup

Before

Having a taste of the grilled cheese!

How damn hard is it to meet

This simplicity!

The Expected reject of Expectation

Peace out

Sat myself down in the back row

Watched the preacher load a bowl

His Proclamation

"God gave the weed to man, he's going to smoke it!"

This shit is natural, respect that he didn't hide it

Until of course, he demanded ten percent

Twenty Fourth Hour _1

Eyes moving under the lids

Sleeping off this bad trip

Upon this heap of fluff

Just another Twelver

Zero-O-Zero

Meaning for most

Outside world

Rotting in sleep!

Who gives a rip?

A voice whispering messages

Opposite of love

Reversed in tongue

Spiritual riddle

Inside oddities

Room cold

Frozen breath

Immediately crystalizing as it's released

Silver steel in hand

Fingertips, shades of blue

Upon the iced carpeting

Small outline

Infant humanity

Shadow frozen to the wall

Eyes thirsting

Lusting for blood

Seeping sockets

Sucking spiritual cum

Life fluid, running warm in a dead carcass

Darkness spreading

Consuming my everything

Lapping like a stray dog

Hissing

Great the serpent

Sucking fear out of the air

Gaining power

Encompasses all

Inside a shell of sludge

Grabbing upon a face

Penetrating

Down the throat

Up the nose

Removing moisture

Emptying another juice box

Life

Bright is the light

Melting like wax

Arching with power

Inside the God theory

Twenty Fourth Hour_2

Humanoids

Living with one book of laws

One from twelve

Thirteen total

Intelligent cretins

Pretending to know it all

Another worthless Kakapo

Pecking upon the ground

Worms in a beak

Slithering to a grinding death

Out it comes

The white shit

Baking on this windshield

Billion open spaces

No, let's just defecate here

Another tripping event

The worms head all smiles

Traffic madness

Why the fuck haven't we discovered teleportation?

Where the hell is the major leap?

Worthless little Aliens

This example of hell

Sun, upon the face

Feel this, burning bush

Saving from a hysteria

Marijuana

Jesus Christ

Dangling from the rear-view

Religion

Shiny is the lure

Hooking into a soul

Rome still rules

An army of brainwashing

This isn't our car?

Never mind

Scratch it from the thought

Don't attend church

Honestly

We used to go a whole bunch

It ended when the sun set

Exhaled the spirit out

Pale was the new norm

Look at this wasted page Gocni!

Twenty Fourth Hour_3

Do we believe?

Just a happenstance question

Yes, something created all of this

Didn't it?

Mean, if it didn't

Why all the fucking bother?

If someone blows your damn brains out

Does it matter then?

Just a sludge parasite

Worth of nothing

Abort the accident

Why give a moment's thought?

From another aspect

Something created this circus act

Beyond this duplication of civilization

What is inside a church?

Humans, insects, full of it

Dictating the great

How to, on making excuses

No, this isn't our car

Jesus still crucified

He's dangling right here

How one sells the symbol of death

As the symbol of life

Probably, greatest sales feat

EVER!

Worshiping it

Let's just suck that dick

Amazing

Our neighbor

This is her car

We just took it

Wanted to try us out some of this

Sanders with benefits living

Her choice of music

What the fuck is this mule dung lyrical waste?

Eject

Out with the disc

Prehistoric in today's date

Nineteen nineties

A CD

Compact my dick

Entitled

For the fuck of the Call

Sleazy Hurtis Crapmac

Meeting him in a truck stop stall?

God, does he Blow?

Blows

Fucking Gayness

Someone went crazy

Sniffing the fairy dust

Just Kidding, WINK, WINK

Just toss that in the back

How disrespectful!

We understand the concept

Twenty Fourth Hour_4

Hi Jesus

Here, dangling from the rearview

Now winking at us

Bring another

Can't wait for the day

When Jesus comes to collect

That royalty check

One hellacious payment

Time to ante up

Jesus, a household name

Frigidaire, Vizio, GE, Samsung, Jesus Christ

Brought in today's high definition standard

Twenty Fourth Hour_5

VANITY

Just so happens

In a time, like this

We're prepared

ZIP

What are you gazing at?

No, it's not inside our pants

A jacket pocket!

The mind of these silly children

ASTOUNDING us!

A CD

POP goes the ego

Let us try this, please

Some Puscifer up in this

Or is it

Your bitch, up in?

The commodity of luck

"Conditions of my Parole"

Fitting, no?

Screw you Jimmy!

We're talking about

    "Carina Round"

Wait one moment

  A world turning purple

What about

    "Mahsa Zargaran"

That's someone to bite the fist over, is it not?

Ravaging, humanistic beasts

Desiring fleshly hotness

As the sex love floats from luscious lips

Damn the sound

Where in the hell we going?

All these damn questions

Just driving

Listening to the......

Our neighbor, doesn't give a damn

She's dead

Laying in the bed

The dog

Upon the floor

The stench

Nauseating nostrils

Making the stomach churn

One might label it puke

Should probably tell somebody

Constantly

Do the right thing

Bangs at the door

Another loner, creeping the world

Least she died on her terms

Glad we could borrow the car once more

Listing to this apologetic tune

Thanks Jimmy for redeeming the world

Really, just going to Ralphs, aren't we?

RIGHT!

Having a bad case of the munchies

Inhaling euphoria

Smoking a giant green dragon

Contorting the mind

Twisting the illusion

Reprogramming the essence of being

Seeing real once again

A world

No longer living for a review

One care, having not!

Opinions, the shit from minds

Protruding themselves

Difference of none

In likes with a juicy log

Slithering out of the anus

PLOP

Stained water, dripping off the ass cheek

Time to wipe

This making of nonsense

Undecipherable

That is

For the common folk

Looking to elicit some flesh based emotion

'Fuck you!'

That's rude!!

Programmed, one single "train of thought"

Repeating steps

Living the tale of another ant

Marching the same path

Day in, Day out

Off "IT" goes

Can't tell you how grateful

Oh, the love

Gratitude for this moment

No expression counts

We are floating along

Together

Here we are

Twenty Fourth Hour_6

Time to feast

Once more

This battle

Digesting animal flesh

Fulfilling the need

Living plants

Manmade toxicity

Down it goes

Hole to ingest

Through a tunnel

One might grasp it as intestines

Casing for the wiener

Transformed

Converting to human waste

From light to darkness to light

The best time to read this

Dropping a load

Nature

Pesky is the rule

Losing thy way

Back to the twelve

Resting on the fluff

Meticulous thy mind

Placing Gocni back in a cage

Removing

Artistic voice

Closed

Be back at Noonish

To do it again

Upon the morrow

When the crow indicates

Time for another bad trip

Shall it be

Just another slave

Inside the Grid

For you, I do bring this joy

Two faces close

Their breath

Penetrating skin

Peach fuzz raised

Tingles raining down the spine

One is married

This action, a sin

Pope will cut off thy head

Lips, desiring to touch

Help, feel the desire

Moral code

For now

Needing to be placed aside

Tearing off the clothes

Needing nakedness

Closeness

Dig inside

Fill the void

Lips connecting

Flames engulfing

Hands clenching

Bound, as the passion forms

Electricity, as the soul's merge

Two voices

Two Minds

One Body

Lusting love

As the nails dig

Peeling back the skin

Sweat mixing with blood

Pulling hair

Almost snapping the neck

Hands grasping the throat

Choking

Slapping the face

Stabbing skin with a burning candle stick

Into the abyss, we went

With the condition, of

Emotional semblance

Brought about at the Twenty Fourth Hour

Signing off

The good Doctor

The Experience

It's a unique situation

My life that is

As I surpass my ten-year mark

In an industry that's fairly odd

Always treated as some overhead

Some god damn ring worm

Sucking the company dry

"GOD DAMMIT GOCNI, WHEN'S THE BLEEDING GOING TO END? Huh, WHEN?"

VP's would love to squash it

Yet, without it, the company would fall

Note: I didn't say "fail!"

Always, always work around's

As I climb the ranks

The blessing of this career

How high you go, really, up to you

Not what you know

No, rather, who you blow.

I make a decent living...now

Hasn't been that way in a long time

Don't find myself shopping at box stores

Ironic, when I made less of nothing

Trying to shop cheap

Couldn't afford mom and pops

Box stores or bust baby

Twenty dollars must last the week

Now though, I shop mom and pops all the time

I don't know if the reasons

Because I can afford it

Or perhaps

I want to ensure they keep their doors open

I find myself anti box

Yet, I know where I came from

The box is needed

Broke mother fuckers running around

Just like I was

It's not their fault

Wasn't really mine either

It is hard to climb out of nothing

I know, speaking from experience

"What, did you climb Mt. Everest or something?"

No, I was in a pit

Not on top of a mountain

Where did you come from?

"I came outta your mom!"

Well, you're a rude one

Here's a quarter

Make yourself useful

Go play in the road!

Sorry about that!

As for my current career

Wasn't always the case

A welder for quite some time

Made an OK living

Not at first, no way

Eventually made top rate

Ten years eventually

Body half broken

No more raises

"Gocni, you did really good this year,
Here's that Atta-boy I told you about
You're as high as you go.
Want a tootsie roll?"

Don't you love that?

I sure do!

The end of the road, with only a tootsie roll to show

Nothing more to strive for

That was me

Road Closed

You done seen the end of the horizon

"You could have just gotten a different job, you're LAZY!"

True, Had two cars, house and family

That would have to go as well.

Not the family part

It got so bad at times, the boredom

I'd ask for different tasks

Sometimes the SUP would give me them
Like candy at the end of a shotgun

Knew he got a power trip from it

I'm quite grateful for Two Thousand and Eight

"Stupid Gocni, grateful for one of the worst times in history and its Two Thousand Eight fool!"

Yeah, that's right, grateful and I like the way it sounds

With the "and" ya twat!

Let me explain

I worked

Owned a house

Was irresponsible

Borrowed, more than I should

Did things without calculating consequence

Built my house on sand

Right in the path of the waves

In the blink

Gone

My job flew the coop to China

We probably would have survived

But we just finished a war with Leukemia

It drained everything we owned

Hence, why we borrowed off the banks shit

Try surviving on one income with a family

It can be done but not while owning a house

Not while having a limited job

Hell, not even while working two jobs

Not sorry about any of that

No complaint department here

Really a looking point

Divorce was inevitable

We never grew together

A constant split

Not apologetic about that either

Shit happens, show me the guarantee

I've yet to find one

Religion is another man's dream

I did something though

Over paid to go learn

Just a certificate school

Really, have no use for school

Takes the adventure out of doing

Being instructed how to behave

Communicate

Shit, how the hell does one make it

Without effective communications

I don't regret doing this either

Opened another chance

What really makes America great

Chances after you fail

There was a period I lived on the streets

Didn't have nothing

Not a penny

The reality of it all grew extra big

Roots kept me planted deep

Fear ruled this conscious state

Those evil voices, proclaiming me to be

Rotten nothing

This darkness, lingered for seven years

Mental assault, difficult to bear

Suicide a daily thought

Just can't do it

Ending it all doesn't compute

Need to see how it works out

Like a damn movie

Should ride this to the end

Pulling myself out

Didn't come cheap

Cost, everything has one!

Time, energy, health, beliefs

The price of admission

Occasionally, I'd get the religious fanatic

Telling me everything will be OK

All part of some, God plan

The selling point

"PURPOSE"

That used to piss me off

Don't go pissing on me

When I'm down in the muck

Rarely seeing three feet ahead

Others run you over with their feet

"Back down with the filth."

You can just see the negative energy now

Well, maybe you can't, but I can

Lived it I guess

Wrong way of thinking about things

Not going to beat myself up over it

Done way too much of that

The Experience Needed!

Saved me

Made me appreciate what I had

The Experience

A highlight of my life

Period I have learned to cherish

When I was in the fire

Understood I could make it

Torment caused me to gain vision

Into a new form of maturity

I see this world

With a new light

I don't need material possessions to make me

It's not about what you do for a living

To hell with fancy titles

Marriage isn't for everyone

Does anyone really need white picket fences?

Maybe, some do and that's cool

I don't

It's OK to have all of that

For me though

Discovered I was nothing more than a slave

Owned by it

When the possession dictates it's too valuable to lose

Then the realization is that the possession now rules

Oh, suppose, someone is wondering

How I pulled myself out of the pit

Simplest thing in the world

Transparent

Why it's hard to find at times

I stopped caring about it all

Came to terms I was no longer in control

Just tossed it

Packed my bags

Found another State to call home

I was ridiculed for doing it

The standard topic

"You'll never make it!"

Everything was said

They just didn't realize

I had nothing to lose

Dangerous

Still

A new beginning

Suddenly, I found, nothings impossible

There is, a chance in hell, that I can make it

This was discovery again

How weak and dependent I became on others

No wonder my spirit was dying

Why I felt so weary

So yes, I am grateful

For two thousand and eight

No, I won't type it correctly

Get over it or go read someone else's shit!

Been prospering since

Saving money, zero loans

Nothing new

Just good enough to make it around

Investing wisely

Be the smarter clown this time

Not playing the spoiled American fool

Amazingly this country didn't learn

The big deal effected everyone

Yet, the ones hit hardest

Twenty percenters

The broke class

Banks still fudging the numbers

Why not

What do they care

Taxpaying chumps had to pay for it all

Walking off, bonuses, lining the pockets

Damn

Well, they knew the system

Played the game

House never loses

Gambling, the whole system rigged

Way I see it Jim Bob

When you go through life

Making mistakes

It's alright to make mistakes

Where the problem is

While going through life

Making mistakes

Never maturing from them

Learn and grow went out the door

To do it better on the next turn

Lessons of value

Discovered during one of the greatest defeats

A motto I hold dear

Rise, Try again

Never quit, thanks again

He was screaming from the curb
This guy
Calling me an asshole
While on his bicycle
I just listened to his commotion
Something about me not stopping
He kept saying it
Over and over and over again!
Asshole
I just smiled and waved
It could have been so much more
Should have made it more entertaining
But I was just an asshole
Who didn't stop
Listening to a bicyclist screaming

Oblivious to the World Around

Purposely seeking

Exploring closed doors

An innocent roams the halls

Coming into its own

SILENCE

"Moises, who's the guy walking onto the stage?"

Not sure

"He's wearing a mask."

I see that

"Where is Johanna?"

Went to get a coffee

"Is this one of the speakers?"

Must be, he's on the stage

"How do you know it's a man?"

I don't

"Should I record then."

I guess so

"Really wish the coordinator just didn't up and disappear"

IN FRONT OF A MICROPHONE

What Shall I talk about?

Perhaps, I will treat this like meat

Soak it, with a good serenade

Tenderize, with my neighbor's skull

Oops, sorry Jim Bob

Though, this sure isn't some musical

Won't be a romance novel

Be I, not a lover under your window

Caroling, fare thee wells, beyond twilight

No, rather, I be not!

Thither thou yonder

Away, with these, idioms of thought

Ahh, hell no, this is a bore fest!

A real snoozer

Shits for free

It shouldn't be good

Should be just barely passing

Like a Grade D meat

Toxic Bell anyone?

Though, I'm not one for writing trash

Even though, some professor

His name, wasn't Tim or anything

Never did he state, my writing, comparative to shit

"You stick to sweeping floors Gocni, leave the writing to the professionals!"

Laughter, from the student masses

As I was shamed away

They all just pointed at me

Ridiculed me, for creative thought

I wanted the pain to stop

One step off a tall building

Down to the ground

Ending it all

Must be fun, living inside the box

Another monkey

Beautifully teaching other's

On how to be monkeys

Residing, at the local brainwashing academy

These two feet

A blessing to carry

Bringing me to many new places

SILENCE

"I don't know Moises; this guy doesn't fit the motivational mold."

Not my job to decide that

"It doesn't feel right man; should we call security?"

Not in my pay scale

"Johanna isn't going to be happy with this."

Guess he shouldn't have left

AT THE MICROPHONE

I write, because I love it

Thanks a lot

Though, what you think of it

Obviously

Is for you

If you think I care

I care not!

It's not arrogance

I'm not some wormwood twat

Writing, keeps a gun out of my mouth

This world, unbearable

No, I'm not mentally insane

Certified crazy, sorry, please try the next-door down

No Wilfred

Not the old lady!

We all know She has twenty cats

It's her fight against loneliness

Her family, no longer comes around

The next door damn it

Yeah, that's it!

What an anus

Feeling a little lover boy

Perhaps, no, not at all

I'm just a guy

Not ordinary by any imagination

Skipping along

Who's seen, more than enough

Been watching society

For ages now

Bloody savages

Silently studying

Circus chimps

Civilization slowly disintegrates

All these new and special groups

Dullards of ill tongue

Talking some utopia nonsense

Little darlings

Wanting an equal turn

Driving a train

Filled with nukes

Hit the button Henrietta

Time to meet the lord

Its times like these

We should all just wear a hangman's halter

Say Good bye, cruel world

Sit inside the bathtub

Slit the wrist

Escape as we don't exist

This life, illusionary dung

TWO IN THE AUDIENCE

"Psst, hey Julia, who is this guy?"

I don't know, he's not on the list

"I'm not feeling very motivated"

Me either

"Where is the Seminar leader?

How would I know

"My psychologist told me attending this convention would be good for me."

I was told this would help boost my sales

"This speaker is talking about ending life."

Disturbing

"I can't handle this, I need to leave."

Are you OK?

"No, I'm shaking, I need air."

Alright let's go

"I think I'm having another breakdown"

BACK AT THE MICROPHONE

Not funny, I know

Yet, I find myself happy with the thought

Really, not a pleasant sight

This isn't stupidity

Others have been noticing

Shit, I think they have

Some bold souls

Possibly?

Trying to save it

It's good of them to try

Speaking up

The system is rigged

No shit, you don't say

Wanting more

We need more buckets here!

They just can't perceive

The bow, already under the sea

My goodness, how time fly's

My hands are getting old

A vibe within these bones

Shorter here as it slowly ticks away

Gaze this vast darkness

With a bright light upon my face

Lord, lord is that you?

Hither unto me

Redeem this lost soul

As I no longer feel

TWO IN THE AUDIENCE

"Man, this guy is all over the board!"

He sure is

"Thought this was a motivational convention"

It is, this guy isn't even on the schedule

"Who the hell is it?"

I think he said his name was Gocni Something or other

"How did he get up on stage?"

I don't recall, he just started speaking

"He's deep and all, what is with the mask?"

Not sure, I'm trying to listen.

"It's creeping me out."

I find it mysterious

"Do you like creepy mixed with mysterious?"

Definitely interesting

"Say, after this, want to get some take out, go back to my room?"

Oh, I'm married.

"Yeah, that's not what I asked."

AT THE MICROPHONE

This feeling, deep within

Like that unique experience

From a stranger to a stranger

It's irrelevant if I belong here

I'm going to step through the door

Expand the horizon

Think about, what is

Meditate, on what hasn't come

Contemplate, a greater beyond

In the vastness is a darkness

Like a deep fog

This guy lives there

He never allows me to gaze upon him

He has a bright light

Coolness upon the heat

It moves the fog

I have yet to figure it out

When you go into this place

It's as if he knows you're there

Even though, its pitch black

Can't see another soul

When he speaks

His word is commanding

Yet, very loving

Understanding

Nurturing

A voice that upon first hearing

Is very well known

Like a parent of old

I think he frowns upon me though

Not sure I'm on the list of likeable

I'm probably the pebble that got misplaced

Falling into the air duct

Never to be seen again.

Not much in value

Just a worthless stone

SILENCE

"Excuse me Moises, where is Johanna?"

He went to get a coffee

"Yeah, maybe you can help me then, um, who is this person on the stage?"

I don't know

"My company paid to have its sales force motivated."

I'm sure it will be worked out when Johanna returns

"It better be, or I'm demanding a refund, this is fucking ridiculous, ridiculous Moises."

AT THE MICROPHONE

Seeking

We have men to follow

How unfortunate

Looking for guidance

From a group that has

Zero answers themselves

Maybe, I should write some romance

Not that smut shit

The thought though

Bores me to death

SILENCE

"Moises who's on the stage?"

Dude where have you been?

"I told you I was going to get a coffee"

Well, this guy just showed up and started talking

"Why didn't you stop him?"

How are we supposed to know?

"I think a little common sense would have helped!"

We don't get paid to think

"That's good, it would have been a waste of money if that was the case."

BACK TO THE MICROPHONE

It feels like a have a broken back

The world without a care

People are just little ants

Easily stomped to death

Mindless

SILENCE INTERUPTED

"Excuse me, Gocni is it?"

Yeah

"sorry to interrupt, but where are you taking us with this?"

Nowhere, I was simply talking to myself

"Well, I'm going to need you to leave the stage please"

Oh dear, I didn't even realize

"This is a motivational convention!"

Great, I'm in such a daze, puffing on green

"Please come with me."

ESCORTED BACK TO THE STREET

How did this happen?

Was I transported in time?

Perhaps, this is all just a dream?

Oh well

Let me find an Uber

I need to get to the sea

Hope you enjoyed the read

Smoke some weed

Live in peace.

It just happens sometimes
That you lose yourself within yourself
One of those great mysteries.
I smoked the pot
Just didn't inhale

President Bill Clinton, the greatest, as far as I'm concerned

Going to Buy a House

It was a voice like no other

A hope during a storm

No, it was nothing at all

There was no hope within the storm

Reality

The ship went down

Stranded, on some foreign shore

I didn't have no Mr. Wilson

Having nothing, while living on the curb

But today, I laugh

Over yesterday's misery

Wanting to saddle a white horse again

This guy has been looking at houses

They're astronomical in price

Take an average Joe a lifetime to pay off

I have some bumps in the road

Crawling out of a devastation

My life was wiped out

I attempted to do everything right

Yet, I was a fool that paid the price

Took the monkey a while to realize

Shit, this is just a gamblers game

Nothing is real

Ideologies are fake

Humans, speak from both side of the face

Waving as they smile

Flipping you off just the same

Gettin our kicks

Living life from some mobile device

Government doesn't serve the people

It owns them

Currency, it's worth, comparative to ass wipe

Here, this fool has been feeling down this whole time

I don't want to own a house again

Want to crawl into that hole and die

Another failure, simply worthless

No Way in Life

Fuck, you'll never own it anyways

When you die

Who cares about all of that

Besides

Someone will be there to steal it

This Ol'Coon

Wants to buy a house

It has a little for money

It goes to work and all

It got back on its feet

It didn't need to be told

It just does

Sure, isn't made from writing

God damn undervalued

Writing these days

Can buy that for Ninety-nine cents

There is a billion people in the world

Writing

Its Ninety-nine cents on the Amazon

Hmmm, if it's good

It doesn't sell for no ninety-nine cents

"Well look what we have here boys

Guess who went and got off track again!"

Writing isn't the point of this, gibberish

Let's not, get, carried away in a tangent

Life is living in Vegas

Constantly gambling on some big break

One into Two

Two to Three

"That's great I'm winning"

No, that's what you're spending

Betting against the house

"Who's the house in life?"

Everything that is against you!

A government that owns you

Corporations that market you

Entertainment that ensnares you

Religion that controls you

Then the day to day's

Health, disease, poverty

Time, all we got boss is time

This clown

Going to sit at the table

With one twenty-dollar chip

I don't have a pot to piss in

My credit...shit

I hope I can fix

Who cares

Now, it's time to bullshit

If we lose this time

Least now we understand

That this imagination is nothing

Just a fool living a great working of fiction

Let me shoot some craps

Maybe win big

Oh, hi Hillary

Didn't know you played this game

Oh, you own it

What if I win?

"What difference does it make!"

She really does give great advice doesn't she!

Then me favorites, we have the whole deal of

No one will give a damn anyways

On average

A life is only remembered for three generations

After that

Its but a forgotten melody

"Bullshit Gocni, I AM FAMOUS!"

Yeah, great, famous

A picture will be remembered

Maybe the color you displayed on TV

Perhaps in some art piece

That's it

Who the hell you were as a person

Apart from that mask of fame

No one will ever know

That will be forgotten

Just like the rest of us

Rotting in the soil

"Now Gocni, I did my family tree."

Great, tell me about all those people

"Well, I can't, but I know who they are!"

Quit your lying

Quit your trying

Knowing them almost an impossibility

Unless of course

You found a journal

Gaining some insight into the mood

During eye slitherin the written text

Still, that isn't knowing someone

"Gocni, you monkey, imitating a fool."

NOW THAT IS AMAZING

"You're crazy."

No, I'm not crazy

It's just one of those deals

"Man, alive dude, what is your problem?"

Nothing, just going to purchase a house

Call it

Mission Impossible

Label it

Fuck it, why not

Market it

You too can own a piece of beautiful

The time is now

"No, god no, not John Hogan Cena!"

What, you can't see me, Brother?

It's all good

Well time to smoke a little

Contemplate why I should

Then write about it

A beautiful blue sky

Give it some fluffy love

Toss a rainbow around by the nuts

Glue a horn to a white horse's head

Take it on a ride around town

Cause this magic

Is what I'm selling for forty large

No, it's not ninety-nine cents

It's time to buy a house

I found one in Compton

Sorta new to California

All my co-workers say it's awesome

I had a feeling they're lyin!

Tomorrow, I'll go and check

This cracka is going to buy a house

Peace

Nothing Wrong with A Little Dreaming

Motionless

A piece of space debris

Floating

Another marble tossed in a wheel

Damaged

Lost inside a mind of chaos

Arrival

The bright light

Enter

A planet floating on wings

Oh, hey there kids

Didn't see you inside the bushes

Why are you hiding?

Who told you that you're naked?

A snake did!

You don't say

Yikes, wait what!

You ate what?

An apple.

Why didn't you listen?

Are you seriously blaming the woman?

That's real stand up of you

What the hell, now it's because of a reptile

You blame a snake

You blame a woman

Who made the decision?

Now I'm to blame!

It was called free will

Don't look at me like that

Shit, now I have to make you some clothes

Can't have you walking around with leaves

You didn't notice that was poison oak?

Yeah, it's going to itch

Dumb SOB

All you had to do was watch the animals

Was that too much to ask?

You're only twelve

That doesn't make it right

Look at you

So, dirty

Time to take a bath

Yeah, going to have to clean yourself

Here, wash with this soap

No, you can't come into my ship

Why?

Oh, I don't know

Because you broke the rules

Destroy the snake

Might as well

What difference does it make!

Well this was productive

Where I'm going?

Getting the heck out of here

No, you go roam the dirt

Should have known better

Yeah, ya should have.

Bye, I'll be back to check on you

See what has become of this fine decision making

Years

Ages, as the time goes

Period

Similar today

Wonders

Man, has made remarkable feats

One air plane

Chasing two balls

Blazing across the sky

A pilot speaks into the mic

No, Sir, they're unidentified

Out maneuvered, that's putting it lightly

I can't even get a lock

Shoot them with the machine guns?

Yes, commander, I'll try

Rounds just bounce off sir

One Disappeared.

I don't know how it disappeared

Not just seeing things

One second it was in front of me

Then it was gone

Oh, shit

Its behind me

I can't shake it

My system is malfunctioning

What's that bright light?

Commander its...

Silence over the radio

Not inside a cockpit

Screams of panic

Fear engulfing conscious

Light that burns

An airplane disintegrates

Flesh melts off the bone

Skeleton sails through the air

Eyeballs

Viewing a new version of hell

Suddenly, vaporized!

The ground trembles

Men of valor

In a fit of disturbance

Thousands of planes take off

To destroy the unknown

A new type of war

Rockets launch into space

Logical

Screw it make them nukes

The standard mental retardation

Fingers

Playing with things in the air

Medication

Enough to piss your pants

Sitting in the corner

Locked away in a strait jacket

Out of scope

Crazy is the woman

It's coming

No, no don't say that

I'm not talking to myself!

You can't see them because your blind

I'm not crazy

Don't give me meds

No, I am not making a scene

Listen you mother fuckers

Fuck, fuck, fuck

I will cuss and swear

You'll make me care

I'm on death row

They're coming back

No, no don't touch me

You're all going to die

I've seen your flesh

Wiped clean off your body

Why don't you listen to me?

No, I'm not going!

Don't put me in the padded room again

Was trying to warn you

Not fit for society!

Please, don't increase my dosage

Listen to me, no, no, don't inject me, listen

These guys are real

Show yourselves

They're going to ki……

Its silence once again

Night

Cruising at the speed of light

Some

Proclaiming it's the gods of time

Others

Just a shooting star

It doesn't matter

The unidentified

Crashing into the earth

Shirtless women

Laying on their faces

Insect creatures

Causing a mass epidemic

Orgy of death ensues

Steve, Jeffrey and Thomas

Entering the scene

With some tag, along

We'll call him Bobert

They were just following their phones

Chasing some stupid Pocket Man

It was just me

Waking up at three fifteen

Nothing wrong with a little dream.

No Love for Self

I've walked a lonely world

What feels like millenniums

Upon shoeless toes

Searching, like a featherless bird

Seeking refuge from a raging storm

All alone, no foreseeable purpose

Filled with that desire

Given to visions

Dreams, like floating balloons

Deflated and sent to the ground

Just walking in an empty world!

I was that solo sailor

Two oars with a small mast

Floating on the face of a god

Nothing but openness

A vast endless hope

Longing to be on a shore!

And in that longing, wondering

A sailor in love with his ideas

Something he believed in

Till hope faded

Hopelessness crept in

Adventurer was I

Seeking places of the worst type of treasure

Massing things that faded

Like that of a leaf

Before the long winter sleep

Standing with eyes in the heavens

Walking tall and righteous

Valor filled eyes of greatness

Exploding like a bright star

Worn out adventurer

Older than his time

While giving nothing

Digging for wealth

As the bottom falls out

The world has crumbled

I was a survivor

Beaten to the grave

Broken meat

Wasted, not defeated

Mind in a wicked cave

Dark clouds around a body

Life drained in that moment of pure emptiness

Great pain, thy greater misery; heartache!

I've taken a walk on lost trail

Feeling nothing inside

Painful emotions

Subdued with a fiery rage

Running scared

Beaten and neglected dog

To be careless to morals

While Loving something

No love for self

Dark light reaches out

An Imitation white.

Believe to be deceived

Deception, does it ever leave?

I've created the world's greatest dream

Imagined in my head how it should be

I did not waver, nor doubt

Just believed

I commanded you to me

Summoned you without your knowing

I was the white knight from your dreams

Loving you beyond imagining

I created the you, in us

Delivered what you desperately longed for

I was the dark that was within you

Bringing you to ruin

I am the loss you'll remember

Down with the Middle Finger

I'm down with a middle finger

Better a fist

Real writing here

No rift playing

I don't give a rip

What skin you linger in!

Change your drawers

Don't ya?

Best wiping front to back

Other way around?

Who the hell knows

Made you contemplate!

It's your damn life

The point, too many rules

Do this, don't do that

Correct for the incorrect

Twisting our minds quick

I'm in likes with the art

Ya, ya, it was Lucifer, glad you caught that

Fuck that clown

So many fools

Running around, with a hand over their eye

Selling no talent

Pretending the thug

Backed by paperless worth

Here, have some ass wipe

It's almost designer

Comes in George, Abraham, Alexander and Andrew

I'm down with a middle finger

Better a fist

Rage me a Rebel

Love of fun guns

Bang, bang

Screwing imagination to paper

Keyboard, pen, brush

All good!

My age, Gen-X

XXXXYYYYZZZZ

Put my ass ta sleep

Not into the LABELS

Market me some debt

That's Societal elite

Dangling dolla bills

Off the end of a shotgun barrel

Separating the cattle

These to the slaughter

Those to the white picket prison cells

A free person

Sleeps on the curb

Walks the streets naked

No rock bottom fucks given

Modern slaves looking around

These cocksuckers ain't buckled down with chains

That's no way to safety

Bad trip to contemporary cotton picking

Who be the fool?

Nine to Oblivion

Babies raised in scarecare

Wondering if there will be a job tomorrow

Living for another man's cock size

The broke asses

Yeah, they ride the bus

Zilch high flying Ferrari's

Depending how hard they hustle

They may get to eat day old sandwiches

Seen the down

Be kinder humans

Not owned by?

Use your mind!

Nothing left to lose

Give out half what they got

Thinking about fellow man

Who really is the savages in merry land?

Back on track

Went off the beaten path

Look for that SAVIOR in the clouds

That's him on a stage

Or is it her

Shit, it's Godernment

Does it matter?

Maybe it's a robe

Hiding behind the Crucified Souls

Talking some gibberish

First collecting a check

That's them in a MaNsIoN

Faithful still in rags

Slaves endlessly bashing each other

More like New World Order cave dwellers

Swinging bones, cracking skulls

Once again, we kick it to you

Over some bullshit ideologies

Who actually writes this D rated horror flick?

Time for a blender

Stick your head in

We find the brain yet?

Lab rats craving heroine

Never once do we learn

Dogs just chasing tails

Round and round

Repeating the same bullshit

What skin you linger in?

I don't give a rip

No rift playing

Real writing here

Better a fist

I'm down with a middle finger

Café Conversation

At the end of my life

Contemplating the point

Inward the conversation

Life, how it just goes

These hands, old

Worn thin

Things they've done

The young gal behind the counter surprises me

"How ya doing sweetie, want a donut?"

She refills my coffee as I shake my head for no

Odd she is

Odd, the times these days

Colored pictures all over her skin

Holes the size of quarters in her earlobes

How things have changed

On our way to the end

Personal Armageddon that is

Television playing the news

Another bombing, fifty people dead

Always the same form of tragedy

Bell on the door chimes

In walk's two Young Bucks

First dressed nice

Second dressed like shit

They sit at the counter

Small talk with the waitress

Small talk, not worth mentioning

She pours two coffees

Places the order

Contemplation in my brain

"How long have I been doing this?"

Far too long, far too long Skip

Take a good long sip

Warm feels refreshing

Young Bucks blabbing

My ears still work

Still at this age, observation, first rate

Young Buck One calm in demeanor

"Where's the package?"

Young Buck Two fidgets nervously

"First the money?"

Pulling out envelopes

Passing them, attempting to be secretive

Very inexperienced, failing miserably

Young Buck One starts to open the package

Young Buck Two grabs his hand

"What the fuck dude!"

Young Buck One pulls his hand back

"Received a good amount of money here, I have to verify this is real."

Young Buck Two with intense emotion

"Can't just open the package mother fucker, they're watching, they're everywhere. Ya don't grasp what this is?"

Young Buck Two stands up

"Listen, people have died over this!"

Young Buck One doesn't seem to like that
"People died! What people? Where you going? I have Questions, that I need answered!"

Young Buck Two doesn't seem to care

"Fuck off, I'm outta here. They'll come, they'll come. Know what's good for ya, run!"

Young Buck One doesn't fathom the seriousness

"Hey, need to explain this, need to sum up a report! This needs to be documented. need help."

Young Buck Two heading out the door

"Screw that, I'm gone, know what's best, you'll do the same. People are dead, I witnessed it!"

Running out the door as if the place was on fire.

Chimes echo as the door closes

Another chapter over

Young Buck One opens the package

Contents of the envelope sliding upon the counter top

Flash drive, photos with miscellaneous items

He unfolds what appears to be

A blood-stained piece of paper

Kurt

Don't cry my love, I'm alright, everything is fine
If you're reading this, I'm dead. Don't focus on that, please focus on what I sent. Make sure these contents are received in the right hands. That my death, my work, was not in vain. Burden of what remains, my work, my legacy, truth. Most importantly, the truth of what I helped create. It will be hard, things of this nature are complex for the human mind to comprehend. The DNA samples, the flash drive, key to the lock box, all provide the details, the evidence. It's often stated, that if it's too good to be true, it probably is. Although, what is out there, only a select few

truly know. Listen to me, it's all true, all of it. Nations have had exposures; people, brave enough, to come out with the truth. They were silenced, relatively quick. The world doesn't believe, it can't believe, it's not allowed, all of it is controlled. My God Kurt, what have I done! The ones that are in charge or believe they are, will not tolerate a collapse in their well-designed system. Not talking about Governments, they're just part of the system that was created. This is much bigger in capacity. This is the truth! Understand, that right now, your life is over. I'm truly sorry my love, though, what you hold, they will kill for, kill, to make silent. I'm sorry! I kept us a secret, not to guess, though rather, they already know who you are. They have ways beyond the scope of man. Whatever happens, they must not recover the contents. Right now, flee, take nothing, get off the grid. Destroy anything electronic, anything with an RFID. Go to the mountains we visited in Greece, stay there, a young man will find you, he'll wear a turquoise vest. Give him the package. This must be exposed. Nothing else matters. You're now responsible for the future of humanity.
Be safe Kurt, I'm sorry, you're the only one I ever trusted, only one,
I ever loved.
Wish I could have touched your face.
Trust no one, keep your head down.
Sincerely my love
Dr. Jan McAllister-Shroud

Young Buck One laughs while shaking his head.

Mumbling

"I think I was just scammed."

While sliding the contents back into the envelope

Always goes quick

Peering into my half empty cup

Its deep inside my own hell

The waitress walks past

One plate of eggs, sausage on the side

Small talk about the guy that left

Small talk, not worth mentioning

Looking up, she is refilling my cup

I'm in a daze

My life, aberrant

Old, too old for this shit

Young Buck One walks past me

Observing him as he enters the latrine

Coffee black like my soul

It's suddenly time, taking a long swig

Toss a few dollar's down

It's called a TIP

Time to punch the clock

Walking to the latrine

Gloves, covering old worn thin hands

Gently open the door a crack

Eyes observing all

Young Buck One is taking a piss

Quietly stepping in

Still not making sounds

Politely tap his shoulder

Young Buck One in a sense of shock

"I'm going to the bathroom sir, wait your turn!"

He turns his head giving me a look

The look of annoyance

Just enough

What I need is exposed

Clenched hand, mastered tool worn thin

The hook, lands perfect behind his ear

Out he goes

Falling like a tree

Grabbing him

Dragging his lifeless body into the stall

Suddenly my age shows, out goes the knee

Damn my fist hurts

No patience for this

Pulling out a syringe

Poking it under the finger nail

In seconds, his body convulses

Bad was the movie

Scene played over countless times past

A war to keep things secret

It's over, he's silenced.

Sliding his pants to his ankles

Removing the package

Contents secured

Taking his wallet

Driver's license states his name was Jeff

Journalist card

Picture of wife and kids

Haunting it is

Four fifty in cash

Another shame

Fools believe in the game

Placing the wallet back in his pocket

Picture left in his lifeless hand

Least I could do

His face contorted

Eyes towards heaven

Coroner will call it, cardiac arrest

Always the same

News will call it another tragedy

Close the stall door

With magnet, sliding the lock

Status, Red, In-Use, do not disturb

Stopping at the mirror

My face, old, wrinkled

Nothing within

Excuse I use

For the better of National Security

The greater good

Shit no longer works

Been in the business for years

Door opens, my body in defense

Some redneck walks in

"Is someone in the stall?"

Just shake my head

He goes on about how he has to take a shit

I don't care, just my face in the mirror

My face, no soul

Just business, nothing personal

No longer conscious of my conscience

Suddenly, feeling something

Collecting self, programmed justifications

Completing objective

Exiting latrine

Waitress, thanking me for stopping in

Nodding my head

Exiting the Café

The sun, warm on this old face

White car on the street

Passenger side window rolled down

Pulling out "A" package

Walking past, toss it in

Car drives off

Another cake

Walking, endlessly down the street

Personal shame

Keeping things silent

Walking on no Particular Day

Was on a walk, on no particular day

Meathead, down the way, was talking gorilla to a kid.

Wind picked up, tumbling a box down the street

Wondering about the contents

Meathead, still blaring away

Kid whimpers in sheer defeat.

Got me to thinking about the world

Contemplating my book!

This is the story from the event.

A box at my door

Screaming to be opened

Twelve by twelve in size

Titled: Miscarried Dream

Sender: Unknown

Recipient: Disenchanted self

Taking hold an infant on the floor

Holding snug against the chest

Little hands, clenching, for life

Walking down the hall all smiles

As if a confident teenager not altered by life

Doors, doors, doors

Rows upon rows of doors

One Eight Seven mine

Lazy, fat ass on the couch again

The Debby Downer looks at me

"What's in the package?

Pay no mind states my personal insanity

"Hey dumb fuck, I'm talking to you!"

Stopping in my tracks

"Sorry Phil, didn't see you sitting there."

With complete disgust, he gets up

Time to play the in your face game

"You looked right at me!"

Holding my box tightly, the infant, suffocating

"I honestly didn't see you, I'm sorry."

It's the lie of all lies

No care, the guy is a prick any 'Ol'ways

Two inches from my face

Teeth, yellow, hosting something beyond vile

Clamoring brown eyes

Painted by a brush saturated with bile

Soul, long gone without a trace

"Ya calling me a liar?"

World just spins in my mind

Attempting to envision paradise

Breath, just breath

His mouth is moving again

I can see his hate, his distaste in life towards me

Surfing the tsunami about to strike

"What ya got in the box?"

Survival, instinct, mother protecting her young

"Not your concern!"

Not liking that much, no sir

Massive the force

A box he now holds

The baby, violently shaken

Agony fills my throat

Fucking ape stole my life

"What you going to cry?"

Tossing my baby into the air

Laughing while doing it

Cruelest of the cruel

Spinning as it goes

Fiend attempts to catch it

Bouncing from hands when a corner touched down

Horror's, I'm froze to watch

Ripping open as it bounced

The heart scatters across the floor

I fall to my knees

Shadow from a giant darken on the horizon

The Demon Defiler picking up my baby's heart to feast

"What's this? A stupid book! Hey, why is your name on the cover?"

Disbelief defined across that train wreck of a face

"Is this what you do in that room all day?"

Nightmares do come true

When hideous opened my book

"What's this shit?

He loved her, he knew her soul

Though duty called.

War, the greatest of trials.

He within the train, she on the platform.

Blowing kisses, waving goodbye

As the metal beast chugs, away

Chasing each other to the end.

Shouting their endless love.

Endless as tears strike the ground

Giant thumbs, violently handling my love

"This book sucks! Don't quit your day job, oh, that's right, you don't have one. Fucking bum!"

The world shakes as he turns to walk away.

"Oh, here's your stupid book!"

Wrist snaps, it's my baby, sent in flight

Sailing past my head

Banging off the wall

Mayday, Mayday, it's a crash landing

Cover bent, page torn, once new, now ruins

Soft meek hands cradle the remains

Carrying it gently to the sanctuary called room

Watching in agony as it gasps its final breath

It was fucking murder

Now someone has to pay

She was my dream

I used my white light

Purchased like an idiot

They said no

I said yes!

They knew best

I knew shit

Never mess with another man's rhubarb

She Hulk

It began, just as fast as it came to an end

Was one of those, suicidal off the cliff affairs

Another believable ride, noted in the books

Roll lover coaster named Demon Lust

She came off the rails on the final run

Front row idiot, smack in the action

Sending the fictional beast into the flames

She was into fitness

I was into not giving a ripped

Somehow there was chemistry

Human beast Lust, fooling us into the magic love bus

God damn the candy man!

Our single interest, sex, more like getting fucked

As time progressed, she transformed into a rock

It was her thing, made her feel strong, accomplished

Myself, transformed into a lump of befuddled fluff

I fell out of touch, lost to liquid dust

Lying together was quite odd

Her sick pack,

Not the type that belongs upon a clown's hand

It was no longer, comfortable

Being with a woman who resembled a man

Fitness, her twelve-hour affair

Drinking moonshine was mine

Working my own six pack, one bottle at a time

Need to do it better

Flex my liver

Making it a Twelver

Right, bring the keg, no cup for me

Always tired, her ultimate excuse

Hand of mine, calloused from masturbation

Kicked to the curb for a Silverback

Found out via text

Via message

Via greatest of ease

What toxic relief

It was good on my end

Drinking that is

Toasting to the pain that went away quick

Time progressed, feelings, lost, within the next glass

Mary makes everything better in the end

Was informed, the Silverback, hell bent on rage

Knocked her around a bit,

Such a shame

We met out once

Airplane was bouncing all over the place

I ditched the show

Jumped without a shoot

My fitness of fluff saved the day

Bounced like a ball upon impact

Met the guys at the bar

It was the nightlong laugh

I fell off the stool not giving a shit

Condition of My Parole

When I was a dumb youngster

I was kicked out of school.

After my stint in the joint,

it was a condition of my parole to get a GED.

I walked in, put the money down.

The broad in the office, running the circus

Annoyed, that I would just come in to take the test.

"Don't you want to study?"

The shit blurted out of her skunk hole

Simply smiling.

"No, let's just get this over with."

The most appropriate of responses for some worn out

Government worker

She had me sit down

In the shittiest of chairs,

Slamming this book of a test

Giving me a pencil,

Number two.

Back then, it was on paper of course,

I'm old as dirt.

Taking the blasted testing

Math and I, always bitter enemies.

We had a fist fight on paper

I wanted to jam the pencil

Directly through its eye socket.

A good shanking for the cracka.

Obviously, if it had one that is

unfortunate was the time.

I had no idea if I was a victor in the ordeal

Or just received the beating of my life,

Shit gave me a headache.

Any hoot, giving her the damn completed test.

Then sitting, waiting, to hear my fate!

Good thing

I was an experienced clock counter

Literally felt like days.

Finally, she comes out,

Hell, it was more of a waddle.

Zero, absolutely, zero expression on her face.

It was almost as if she was pissed, that I didn't study.

Finally, words slither out of her cesspool.

"Well you passed, here is your diploma."

My only logical response

"Really, I passed!"

Giving me one of those lost sheep womanly looks!

Like, is this little bastard serious?

Probably thinking, he didn't even study!

Paying no mind, she no longer matters.

Taking my diploma from her hands,

Yeah, that is for me.

Smiling larger than life at this point.

Looking at her blank face, into those eyes

That housed the great abyss of Hades.

The great response

"You know, if I'd have known this, I could have saved myself four years of hell, have a nice day peaches!"

I received a diploma

Attempted to go to college

Schooling just wasn't for me

Professors just don't get me

I have no excuse not to succeed

I'm either going to work hard

Or fail from being lazy

Farewell Night Flyer

Farewell, Night Flyer, farewell

To the great mystery, toasting

One bottle of red wine into the air

Sent it sailing, without care

Lasting remark as I embark

Riding this trolley, me this guy

Continually, strolling in circles

There went Uncle Joe, like twenty times ago.

Sure, was a good steward

Here today, gone tomorrow the shit he would say

Momma all medicated, plopped in her night chair

Hardship it is, watching the strong turn frail

Farewell, Night Flyer

It's my son, now a man, should have been there

I've seen my love, stood waiting on the curb

Never had the nerve, not once did I dare

Far away from my worthiness

Battling self-assumable defeat

Riding the ghost of fearfulness

Snorting solid, the white line of doubt

Countless voices of cant's

Pretending to be dearest of friends

Dreams, escaping thy mind

Shadow figures sucking this soul dry

Leaches that have no bounds

Farewell, Night Flyer, farewell

Imagination

Useful tool for a useless fool

Spinning

No stopping this ride

Past, present and the unknown

Shoved into the washer

"Hey, my jeans are in there!"

Not anymore, good friend, not anymore

High speed spin cycle

Every detail mixed together

Bleeding colors

Farewell, Night Flyer, farewell

For on the Morrow, They All could be Gone

There is a great command

Many religions proclaim it

Its listed on their top ten

Thou shall not murder/kill

However, you want to affix it

Meeting some new standard of morals, I suppose

Perceive it black, contemplate it white

This earth, running thick with blood

Ground saturated

I live in a land that proclaims

Being the Greatest in the world

It's boasted like a bright light

On a dark night

Set out to the lost sea

Maybe, someone will perceive

Sure, in the past it might have been

Dependent upon what side the fence

This view is being considered

When it still followed the constitution

Perhaps

It played some form of hero

Now, the role is to play the thug

All about saving lives

Selling bullshit

Delivering the new version of freedom

Some guy, some gal

Proclaiming from a podium

The media reading from scripts

Closing the sale

Got you that new Porsche, Vroom, Vroom

Written off like a bad business deal

Life has value?

Hard to tell!

Estimated two hundred to five hundred thousand

Dead Iraqis

Who knows what to believe

Everything is delivered from liars these days

The price of Freedom

What does it cost?

Ninety-nine cents

At some shitty Dollar store!

Imagine the number

Only six digits

Picture yourself in a city

Back in a time when people

Still said Hello

Men opened doors

Humans respectful, kind to one another

In a sense of the majority that is

Though that wouldn't be real

No, picture it how it truly is

Walking

You can smell the fresh flowers

Scent of fresh cut grass

Voices of children echoes along the wind

While a homeless man sits on the curb

begging for scraps

People just walk on by like nothing exists

Another black man slaughtered because he lives

Newlyweds stroll along the water on a lover's path

Where Natives use to run

A pack of cyclists rushing past

Grandma and Grandpa sitting on the bench,

Feeding pigeons, holding hands!

Cars cruising back and forth

The ice cream parlor full

Humans abroad

A being of the same make

No difference in race

Color shouldn't beget one less

Then as it is

When life is taken for granted

Suddenly, you didn't mean to do it

Another natural occurrence

Blinked, now none remain

Six O'clock news

Vacant was the city

The Media going ballistic

Look at the ratings

Only you remain

Silence, not even a cricket

Just like that, a city of life

Snuffed out as they say

In the blink of an eye

Just corpses

Get it, blink of an eye

What's that?

Oh, not funny!

Wasn't laughing

Spirits flood the eternal plane

They called it freedom

With a price tag

Yet, if we're so hip to liberty

Just for shits

Why'd we let two million die

during the Sudanese war?

Truth is

We don't give a fuck about Freedom

It's the illusion that's loved

What's in it for the US mentality

The deal, play along or get killed

My Land isn't the only guilty party

This shit is spread across the globe

Been happening since the spawn

It's just comical to me

How most don't follow the simple command

We need to go to war Pastor, father, most holy

Give them some shit title

Another man to play the role

Messenger of the Master

Sunday

Now delivered via tele, let us pray

I really like my Bentley by the way

Now it's, Thou Shall Not Murder

You can kill for the greater good.

What is a greater good of killing?

Loosely used like love

Let's get a picture

Shaking hands

Showing the pearly whites

Talking about the Command

It's a lot, way easier, pretending it doesn't exist

Realize, use some common sense

Lunatic Mortals spending more on ways to destroy

Than they do on how to improve

Life that is

Blood runs thick

Mother earth sucks it in

Stars, those eyes of the night, sit pondering

The discussion

What value does human life have?

None that we can see!

Does it have any value at all?

They reverence animals better

A dog runs wild

He's collected

Medicated and healed

Re-homed

The great laugh

A man rots on the corner of Main and Third

No bed except for the concrete

Obviously well deserved

Humans walk on

Eyes fixated on phones

Pretending not to notice

Though, there is no getting around the smell

Maybe that's how we cope with it

Well it's not me, isn't my problem

A ruse to remove some form of conscience

Killing someone's spirit

How mighty

Each day, I feel the earth fade

Like this life force is slowly being drained

How things have changed

Vast the proclaims

On the technological advancements

Look what we did

We need some New World Order

Because we don't have any uniformity

Seems we left behind humanity

This will solve the problem

Blood thickened like mud

Mother earth full

Working, one of the greats

To achieve, promote, grow and learn

Though now, another eternal wait

Taking a walking on water event to get hired

Shit, resources these days, a numbered slave

Have to be next to Jesus Christ

Wearing a fucking leotard

Time to dance fucker, time to dance!

Oh, what's that, you need the job!

Shouldn't be so desperate

Explain this separation gap

Murdering the livelihood

The great command

However, you want to take it

Kill, Murder, what the hell's the difference!

Murder comes in many forms

Drop a bomb

Close a plant

Withhold a cure

Smoke a cigar

Have a party

Give an accommodation

Shit, make it rewards

Financial gains

Don't worry about them

Who gives a shit

Take care of your own

Meanwhile

Blood floods the earth

A Moon rises

Fathers cry

A sun falls

Mothers mourn

Tomorrow, another quarter of a million

To fill an empty hole

Why?

Transgressing a simple command

Take the titles

Remove the lands

Set aside ideologies

Put down the phone

Gaze at the human's around

Each one

For on the morrow

They all could be gone.

Leaving Nothing to Remain

If you come to sit at my table

Taking the food from my plate

It's OK!

Please, take it all

Leaving not one crumb to remain

Better I be

Having an empty belly

Not perverted by worldly things

Never succumbing to dire need

For my food is created daily

Kitchen stocked

Garden well maintained

Every day I eat

So please consume

The food upon my plate

Leaving nothing to remain

I love you
The End

From the Book of Joel 1vs11
Thou shall not steal my style
Or Joel unleashes a payload of ass
Whooping!

Just kiddin you!

I rent this place, pay for it, as if it's my own space! Yet, when my neighbors fuck, I am right there with them. Enjoying the fun! Nothing like sixteen hundred a month and change to live in a place that entertains.

Mommy

A little boy

Did I imagine

Standing on the platform

Smoke billows from a metallic hell

Wheels start to move

Steel upon steel

Grinding forward

The whistle blows

Watching, numbingly helpless

As mommy departs

Phantasmal silhouette

Naught physical

Just a shadow

Seconds into the past

I imagine, a little boy

Walking endless paths

Mother, found inside no other

Not mommy tickling thy tummy

Just a small shoe

Following tracks

Kickin rocks

Towards oblivion

A little boy did I dream

Standing on the platform

Excitedly waiting

Anticipating

Every stopping train

Looking past heads

Yet only he remains

A little boy with dark hair

Sitting in a classroom

Upon an empty chair

Executioner stating his name

Lost to moment

Grades failing fast

No attention given

Just the thought of seconds into the past

I imagine a little boy

Not so little

Standing on the platform

Surveying

Beyond nothing

Mommy, nowhere

Each day

Where the trains used to run

I imagine a little boy

Holding close on the platform

An excellent wife

She understands

Its treated like a date

Same time

Same place

No tracks

Locomotives melted down

Used for buildings now

Just an outline

Resides on the ground

I imagine a little boy

Alone again

No kids

Wife split!

Station transformed into a pub

Filled with life

Street artist captures his pain

Wild tears run the cheek

Yearning for yesterday's dream

Old the gentleman

Wheeled up by a nagging nurse

Gone the time now

Vision blurred

Still waiting

Where passengers used to exit

Wails, from that nagging nurse

That Mommy isn't coming back

I imagine

Just a shadow

Standing on the platform

Peering empty tracks

Always the same

Soul knows

Mommy has made her stop

I wanted the bad girl

I got what I sought

Kicked in the nuts

His Name is Peel

Decades ago

Twas I, a little guy

Straight out of the diaper stage

Mom's fell in love, again!

Another dangerous man

He built me a rocket, we sent it to the moon

Bounced mom off a wall, bought the wrong beer

Took me around on the hog

Mom down a flight of stairs.

Off his lips

Why'd you trip?

There he was, with me, as I caught my first fish

There's moms on the floor

My only murmur

What's wrong with mommy?

He smiles

Oh kid, your mother there,

Intoxicated again
Run along and play.

It was Go Joe time

Glass shattering, screams, the war zone

Damn you Cobra Commander

Off on his Harley

Mom, bloodied in the hallway

Time progressed

National Forest

Took me to the biker fest

Left my mom for another broad

Brought me a comic, knew I'd like this one

His arms around a strumpet, her breasts hanging out

In the open field, he was kind

Teaching me to fly a kite

How it was mighty

Momma kissed me good bye

Peel gathered me from school

His tone, hurried

We have to leave

Sporadically, was I, looking around

Where is mommy?

I remember those eyes

As they looked straight

Void of expression

Lips give a faint utterance

She wouldn't quit, left her for dead, she wouldn't quit

At the house

There he was, packing my clothes

Getting ready to leave on the hog

Some strangers arrive

Four or five

One woman, her name, Barb

Son, you'll need to come with me

Three strangers

Why you fighting with Peel?

Peel tossed in the back of car

We locked eyes

My tears wave

Mothers in a coma

Some foster care

She's gonna pull through

Time went on

Wounds heal

Scars remain

Momma said Peel was an evil man

It didn't register

He took me fishing

Moms stated how he chased us down the road

Was going to slit our throats

But momma, Peel flew me a rocket to the moon

Silence, with talk no more of Peel

Months to years

Home from school

Sitting on the couch

Peel holding hands with mom

Biggest hug from him to me

Reformed

How he was missed

Outside, he taught me to ride my bike

Mom burnt the rice

She got bitch slapped

His voice thundering

Wont you ever learn!

Mommy cries

Peel throwing rice

Moms looks at me

Takes the frying pan

Peel never saw it coming

Momma cracks him upside the head

Down with the giant he went

Not understanding

Momma why'd you hurt Peel?

Peel's an evil man

As we hurry out the door

Drive off into the night

Never to be seen again

Town was new to us

A fresh start

Mom's home from work

Another date she states

Into the mirror

The pretty ones, never learn

His name was Peel

Momma said he was an evil man

It made no sense

He took me fishing

Learned me to fly a kite

If only she didn't burn the rice

Things are going to be different!
When those words are spoken
You know rice is gonna hit the ceiling.

Bored as Shit

I was sitting here

Bored as shit

Just banging away on some keys

Don't feel the seriousness

The stories going to a recycle bin

Want to have some fun

Thought I'd toss the dice

Giving some erotica a quick run

The story

Does it matter?

How about this...

Starting out with some Convict

First day free in ten

Horny was the demon from a cell

Flirting at the bar

Some lonely school teacher

That was an easy choice!

I know, wonderful, isn't it?

She's living on every word

Could have dragged her around on a leash

For Christs sake, just get on with it already

Somewhere in that unconscious state of desperate

She must have believed

This guy needs some saving

They all want to do some saving

She had the tools to change him

He's filling her head

Like a chicken

She's plucking it off the floor

His actions, touching those secret parts

All the good shit of the soul

Way too much to detail

His well-placed vocals

Making her wet

Good god, what is this?

Now she'll need to change those panties

For real?

No, it's a story, shut up and follow along!

She takes him to her place

Smart Men don't bring women to theirs

Naturally, they drink more

Typically, people don't do stupid things sober

Red wine reigns

He drops her shoulder strap

Blouse held by a perky tit

She asks what he is doing

Because it just wasn't obvious

His confidence fills the room

Like that line has never been used!

Taking hold of her

By the neck of course

I'm thinking this is borderline abuse!

Time for some caveman shit

Pound the chest

His eyes just express

I'm doing what I want

Now shut your mouth

Somewhere, he finds a red gag ball

Maybe it was the dogs?

Shoves that down her wind pipe

What's that? You can't breathe?

That's...unfortunate

Pulling out a mile of rope

Was that in the couch?

Hog tied, bound, stuffed

Is she crying?

Who knows!

It's what she wants right

Domination?

Apparently, she just doesn't know it

He rips her clothes off

Hey, that dress costed A buck two fifty.

It doesn't matter, must be rich

It's just a working of fiction

He drops his drawers

Convict is hung like a god

Down to the knees

Get the hell outta here!

Ripped with a six pack, I Suppose

Prison tats galore

Is this guy a gay model?

Her eyes proclaim some tale of terror

Must be enjoying it, right?

A dildo grasped in his right hand

An eight-pound sledge in his left

Where the hell is, he finding this shit?

Going to show the prison life

Driving it in

What the fuck chief

Into the ass hole!

Stuffed like a pig

One swing

Another tap

Damn near exploding

Beautiful blues

Some type of deranged lunatic

The wrong side of Dodge

Who escaped the mental ward?

Likes this type of "Stuff"!

This could go on for days

Bored as shit

I'll just jerk to some porn

Just not on my Facebook wall.

It's easier

Leaving this style of writing to the experts

See you down the road

I couldn't smoke the green stuff
I had to piss in a cup
I degraded myself for paper worth
I needed the money to pay rent
I just wanted to write

Inverse Lucidity

Strolling along

Riding this thing

Call it, a long board

Salty mist

Melting my skin

Children laughing

Ice cream dripping

Imitation mom wiping

Little Timmy crying

Fuck the distractions

Old man walking

Ass exposed

Clothes ripped

Stop to chat

With a real human

Filth perceive another insect

Here is a fiver

Get a meal

It's really from Mike

Paid me for some writing

Riding on

Apes pick things up

Apes put them down

All day long

Fucking Persian

Selling knock offs

He gives me the bird

How I love it

Fuck is the word

Green men dance

Forty for the card

Discover wonder land

Smoke as much as you'd like

Oh, the expense

Adore that

Can I have a sample?

No Free lunch son

Some young doll

Sitting on the corner

Wanting a hand out

No, not today

Tells me to get fucked

Thanks, in kind

That happened yesterday

Onward

This scene

Really want to exit

Same predicament, different date

Mental insanity

A great place

Hiding my ghost

Taking notes

Asians, straight off a plane

Phones, bigger than their face

Blasting pic's

Uploading shit to some snapchat

Someone has to care

Ah, this mortal cesspool

Want to snap this board

Like a twig over my knee

Rip off my clothes

Run free

Display this brain

Tear it from the skull

Connect it to a projector

Disparage my guts

There, now do you see?

A living being!

Some checked box

Not fit for the mandate

Deserves to be shot

No, that's gross

Motion forward

The sun, killing me

Dying of thirst

Dare I drink the water

Is there any left?

Stick a straw into the sea

Suck it dry

I'd unload a bowl of salt

Are you in need?

The Pier

Right said ahead

Public bathrooms

Stinking filth

Humans dropping waste

Ass wipe runs the floor

The heroin addict titled it

Modern art

Look!

Someone lost their shorts

Fucks can find a Nemo

Yet the trash bin

Simply misplaced

Some fool took it home

A souvenir

Everything needs bolts and chains

Barbarians know better

Bubbler

What, water fountain?

Magic liquid dispenser

Does that work?

Am I drinking bleach!

Blah, shit disturber

No, I'm not Canadian

Cock suckers "EH"

Some do that for a job

In these economic times

Born in the land

Upon the place

Where God dropped his drawers

What he left

Worshipped!

Does it matter?

Never welcomed

Where once born

Negativity dislikes change

Nothing, this walk of shame

Looking out

My horizon, endless

Don't have my shades

Some faggot named Pat sang it

Too bad I don't have a gun

Blow my brains out

Paint it all red

This dude

Title it my Lefty

Listening to me mumble

Fishing for something

You alright my friend?

No, glad you asked

I'm dead

Life, meaningless

Speaking cattle

Why we exist?

Let me slit my wrist

Write my name

Desecrate a great expanse

Such a mug

Melody of humdrum.

Oh, that's unfortunate

When I'm down, I fish

Helps soothe the madness

Perfect idea

I haven't tried playing chum

Shove a hook through my nose

Toss me in

Watch me Flop around

Help you catch a Moby Dick

You'll surely make the news

Get to meet some blonde bimbo

With those oversized tits

Marshmallows for lips

Appreciate the niceness

Good day to redress

Not even understanding this sentiment

Forth

Letters on a phone

Dial "infinity"

Just another forty-four

Parallel or a president's ass hole?

It was written

Two for this complexity

A church

Find the Christ in Jesus shoes

On the back of a milk carton

Not holding all the answers

Just what they can make up

Of course, it's in the book

How about this one

Spiritual awakening

Step through the door

Be needing more than dope

Drink the tea

Meet a soul mate

She's single

Her name Flow

Smells of patchouli oil

Nauseating

Great the bush

Covering the legs

Screw this psychopathy

Long board

Setting sail

Once again

Screaming kids

Someone pissed themselves

Mother the hag

Scratching her head

Smack her ass

Don't play like that

Freddy the bum

Eating a sandwich

Thanks again Mike

Back to my beloved

Blanket on dust

Watching the sun

Sizzle the ocean front

Come Along

If you're into crazy

Then please come along

Journey with me

Into the unknown

Back stage of this

Brain

Mind

Soul of stains

Kicking it alone

The usual

Listening to some REM

What is that frequency

Kenny G

No way!

Blasting my mind away

Cheap beer

Call it PB and Rocks

Get me drunk

Counting stars

Pulling triangles

Like some god

I don't have much

Not that its needed

Living in a box

Walking on the moon

Watching time gone

Bye, bye good fellow

There was I

A small child

Innocence for the foul

This human

Can't endure

Sticking needles in the eye

Why little ET?

WHY?

Dumped off into an abyss

Taking a stroll

Through a wild desert picture show

Praising Joshua trees

Ants devouring toes

Let me climb the stairway

I don't understand

Insects

Just trying to get on with it

Tube Television

Broadcasting humans

Searching for Extra Terrestrials

Tall White

Pats my head

Calls me a good pet

Shows me the universe

Teaching me life

Murder

Mayhem

Foolish humanity

Going nowhere fast

It's a hug

Feeling a face unknown

I'm blasting down

On a stolen V Spector Speeder

Screw you and that Extra Testicle

Winds upon my face

Bugs collect in teeth

Millions of zombies

Clapping in the church pews

There's "H.R. Janet"

Preaching

I'll make you famous

Teaching the people

A Subject

Gods forgiving grace

The earth shakes

Sending me off-kilter

As I skate

Giant the snake

Eating Janet

Bye, bye little Miss Perfect

Bye, bye

Was it just a dream?

Giant the crash

Sent back

Was there

Sitting in the rear

She was an elegant speaker

Talking about the wonders

How an abduction

Leads to many things

Her and the crew

Giving witness

Suddenly dead

The whole lots of them

One giant conspiracy

Another accident

OK, let's feed rats

Sitting at the grave

Remembering the face

Those boney little hands

Losing my faith

Death

One

Belief in the unseen

Zero

Don't waste the time

Might as well

Smoke the crack

Fuck it

Heart Attack

Getting on with it

Living in a fantasy

Transforming me

I'll corrupt your state

Cruising in the black and white

One two forty

Speedo not displaying

Screaming the insanity

There's a cricket on my dash

He's chirping in paradise

My guy

He's dressed in drag

It's cool

One of those things

Not drinking the crank

Blown away

Quick hit the lights

Let's catch a perp

Peering in

Watching an elderly undress

Hippity Hop Hooray

Car slams into trash cans

Lights flash

Look, there he goes

This fuck

Trying to run in heels

Told you not to dress in drag

Shit it got away

Call it an easy escape

Captain in a fit of rage

Some form of laughing stock

What he states

Slam a heel in a nut sack

Who's laughing now?

Bitch

Shove a badge up the ass

Enough of this

This isn't me

Remote viewing

Knocking one off at my desk

Just listening to crazy

She's blaring away

A constant nag

What's the problem?

Morning Glory

That time of the month?

Sweetheart

Oh, god the misogyny

Whisky in the coffee

Someone has to pay

Play

Pray

Procrastinate

Shit, is that a knife Kate?

Time for danger Dan

To exit

Life's stage

Such a shame

On the jury

It's not guilty

Dr. Phil-A-phony making bank

Good for him

I'm walking talking crazy

My hands in my pants

Drooling out my mouth

Back in the insane asylum

It doesn't understand the world

Strolling blind in the great unknown

Hell yes, pills!

So as above it is below

Is that the bull?

I'll just give the middle finger

Nut jobs

In robes

Hidden rapists

They're all around

Stealing the world

Good people just wanting to survive

They be wanting dead

While giving head

To some faggot

Named Lucifer

Man, this is excellent meds

Screw this

Time to catch a ride back

Strolling along

In my underpants

People, just don't understand

Maybe it would be better if I had breasts

I'll write circles around most

Sorry

Was just remembering the motto

Be Bold

Just as long as it doesn't, get you walked out the door

This Orange

Taken from a devil's hand

Everyone, give the applause

Take a bow youngster

Back in the diner

Ed's here

I'm in a skirt

Have long blonde hair

My nails painted lime green

Pancakes

Three stacks

Coffee, not black

Time for rectification

He's excited

The moment is near

It's here

The end of the world

Ed, billions will die

Yeah, something to celebrate

Sick bastard

Blood will flow the streets

I'm in a cowboy hat

Tall White

Looks at me

Transcending the vision of cream

Where am I?

In a place time, doesn't exist

Hell, with this

I don't need to see

My face shoved into slime

There it was

LOVE

Remembering those moments

The special times

It came

X

Yet, it also left

Y

Making crafty cards

A greeting of fun

Rocket in the blood

Now none

Waking in my bed

Tall White

Kissing my head

Story

GONE DEAD!

Terminus

Gocni

You guessed it

Doesn't give a damn

Gocni Schindler Presents
Addicts, Aren't We All

Parental Guidance: Foutu explicite!

Bouffées be warned

Dévoué Deux Timmy Le Douche

Never screw with a writer Timmy

Timmy, he's at the store

Just having a friendly conversation

Looking at a Mac Book Pro

The sales clown with a big red nose

Decides to "Swoop in" for an easy "KILL"

Attempting, to sell poor old Timmy one

He's showing the Facebook app

Timmy begins explaining to the sales clown

How Myspace was better

"Remember back on Myspace man?"

He proudly boasts

"When you could have _ _ _ _ ing music on auto-play"

Was so Kool!

So, when you visited the page

My _ _ _ _ing choice of music would play

I sure miss that _ _ _ _ing option

It sucks Myspace sold to the devil

_ _ _ _ing Myspace was way better than Facebook

One irritated Sales Clown honks a gold horn

HONK HONK

"Well that's just a matter of Opinion!"

Timmy is a little annoyed

Who the _ _ _ _ is asking you?

What is that on your _ _ _ _ing name tag?

Did I say, hey, Dick, what's your _ _ _ ing thoughts?

One jumbo gloved finger scratching orange hair

"Well ha-ha I was..."

Timmy all up in arms

You were what?

Sit there and shut the _ _ _ _ up!

What happened to the _ _ _ _ing customer is always right?

Where did those _ _ _ _ ing days go?

_ _ _ _ ing shows how the people

Don't want the _ _ _ _ ing corporation in their lives

Yet, it's there

Scratching this _ _ _ _ing head!

Going bald

Not understanding _ _ _ _!

What the _ _ _ _ is going on!

One clown, one goal, achieve the sale at all costs

Rent surely is due.

Not understanding all the blankety blanks

"Excuse me, this blank and blanking, is that supposed to be the F-Word?"

Yeah, it was, is,

Fuck!

AHHH SHIT!!!

See, look, you fucking made me cuss

Ya stupid ass clown!

A painted face of circles and loops grimaces

"I didn't make you do that?"

Timmy shoving his finger into a red ball nose

Yeah, ya fucking did, Ya calling me a fucking liar chump?

Shoving the finger out of his face

"No wasn't saying..."

Timmy doesn't allow the Clown to speak

What?

I was walking the white and fucking holy

Doing mother fucking excellent

Just received my cock sucking two-week chip

Now, thanks to you, I fell off the fucking wagon again!

FUCK YOU MOTHER FUCKING CLOWN!

I don't even know who the fuck I'm talking to?

Just wanting to achieve a sale, this Clown, doesn't want to deal with the hostility. With improper training continues to dump gas to the fire

"Well I didn't make you use vulgarity!"

Poor Timmy lost in his addiction

Asked me if it was the word FUCK!

What, was I supposed to do, fucking lie?

Now it's my cock sucking integrity that must pay?

Attempting to steer the conversation back to the sale

"No of course not, look at what this Mac Book can do!"

Timmy is all hell bent on rage

Of course, not, I'll shove that Mac up your ass

You're the fucking Kind of scum aren't ya

That would lay out

White fucking lines at a fucking NA Meeting

Then after your cock sucking ass got caught,

Be like, what the fuck, I didn't do anything

Oh, those white fucking lines, no way, that's just

fucking Lik-M-Aid!

We got ourselves

An Honest fucking Lou here everybody!

As the customer's gaze at the marvelous scene a manager's head is peeking around the corner. Poor, poor sales Clown attempts to signal the manager with his eyes to no avail

"Please sir, you're making a scene and no, I don't promote drugs, you're going to get me fired, please stop!"

Timmy just doesn't give a shit, he's Timmy!

Oh, hell no, I won't stop! I'm on a roll thanks to you, seems ya fucking promote vulgarity to a recovering addict

White paint, runs a blue face

"I didn't know you were an addict, I'm sorry, please stop sir!"

Timmy is feeling the flow of his drug

We're an addict!! I am a fucking addict, ya fuck!

Who breeds this fucking kind of stupid?

Tears of pain are beginning to grow vines of rage

"Now sir, belittlement is not necessary."

Timmy hard at it; each swear word, bringing another realm of euphoria to the brain

Sir!! What, is this the fucking military?

Necessary! I didn't think knocking me off the mother fucking wagon was necessary either

Yet, here I am sweetheart, back at fucking zero. Laying on the mother fucking floor

Timmy's hands flail making some gesture of small with two fingers within an inch of the sales Clown's eye

Feeling this fucking big next to the sun

Now, I have to call my cock sucking sponsor...shit!

Seeing an opportunity to dig a knife in the Clown doth strike

"I'm sorry, I'm no addict, but shouldn't it have called the sponsor before deciding to use vulgarity or is it just that stupid and didn't know this?"

Timmy kicks the display knocking some

anti-virus on the floor

Mother fuck what?

Ass hole, you surprised me

I'm only two fucking weeks clean

You Sabotaged my fucking ass for a sale

Laughter protrudes from Purple lips

"Now, I did no such thing you joke of a human being!"

Timmy jams a finger into the chest of the poor Clown

The fuck you didn't

More laughs from a Clown who's had enough

"I'm sorry, I was confused by the blanking and blanks!"

A big red nose bounces off the floor

As Timmy's hand swoops

Sorry, Shut the fuck up with your sorry

I have to call my asshole sponsor

Bitching, fucking cussing up a storm

Thanks to you, ya ass hole!

Probably make the bastard sponsor

Lose his two-year chip

All because of this bullshit!

Smile is what adorns the clowns face

"Sir, you still interested in the Mac Book?"

Timmy losing his mind

Fuck your fucking MAC FUCKING BOOK

SHIT!!!

Where is my phone?...

One Mac Book, call it Pro, in two large stuffed gloves

"No let me show you the Mac Book sir."

Cell phones are out recording

It will be another Youtube sensation

No one really saw it comin

Though, it should have happened moments ago

The arch is wide

Like it was giving birth to rainbows

Hay maker in scope

That connecting smash

Plastic, meeting the jaw bone

Timmy soars

Little pieces of Crapple

Scattered across the carpet

One Timmy knocked out cold

One Mac Book, call it Pro

Dropped on the floor

One said clown picking up his nose

Sirens are in the air

It's just a day in the life of a down and out clown

ADDICTION ISN'T JUST SOMETHING

YOU INJECT INTO THE ARM

Darkness

A father's grasp

Tight against this throat

Choking

Is this a nightmare?

Aware, yet can't feel

Extremities

Conscious, in an unconscious state

Every sound, blasting through a mega phone

Surreal as it pulsates the ear

Invisible footsteps, all around

Dripping water

Rage setting in

Like a vast cloud

End this

Can't speak

Eyes worthless

Can't fucking see

Some grinding noise

What the hell is that?

Motorized

Revving up

A voice

Some shit dialect

Where the fuck am I?

Not able to speak

I smell

The stank

Stinking, like strong copper

What is that smell?

Vibrating all around

Its grinding

Ahh, I see it all

As I die

The hell I made

As they tear me away

Stripping my man hood

Pretty little pink

I perceive you

Walking down the road

Trying to mix

With all the animals

Just doesn't make sense

Wanting to stick your head in some dirt

Lost in this world

I'm the predator, momma warned

Coming to feast, ravenous this bird

Upon that innocent little butterfly

Swallowing it whole

From your dreams

Going to kill that unicorn

While you watch

Slit its throat

Make you drink its salty cum

I have a rope

Darkened, like my coarse soul

Black to cover over that pink

Going to tell you things

Whispering bullshit

Making sweet gestures

Simply, leading you along the way

In that simplistic mind

You'll believe, I am the nicest of all time

In a moment, most vile

Temporarily relate to that pain

Be that white knight

Hitting those precious nerves

Stepping over your knee-high walls

Kicking in that door

While I string, you up

Another insect in this widow's web

Naivety will allow me

Now you can't move

Owning you

I'll deny you the most basic of needs

Making you a slave

To pay my way

Knock you down

Razor sharp words

Cutting that flesh

Hanging you on the wall

Just another painting

We'll call it

ART

Loves will come in

Attempting to strip you down

Take you away

Daddy will shove a finger in my face

I'll make you, feel ashamed

Perverting their goal

You'll push them away

Running to me

All I had to do is look at you

Punish you

Chain you

Whip you

These eyes

Control

Loves try harder

No magic

My will prevails

You'll spit and curse them into hell

This power drives my fire

You take this addiction

To a new level

Now I have no use

Must find another

Your screams, mean nothing

I simply walk off

Launching yourself, desperate

Acting a convulsion on the floor

Holding onto my legs

Door, bouncing off that pretty face

No cares

No concern

You jumped into the abyss

Found you floating

In the great Mississippi

A father's grasp

Tight against this throat

Choking

Smiling while it turns

His statement

A daughter

Innocent little angel

Lost to the fire

Words linger away

Floating this being

Into

Pink flames

Now, I remember

Beautiful thy dismemberment

Welcoming me

Into my resting place

All for daddy's little girl

Who had zero self-worth

I did some hard time you know

I felt I was no good

I wanted to depart from this world

Ya know

I never could muster the courage

Toothpaste Via Mail

Shit time

Greatest ticking of two arms

Cruising a circle of fame

Nineteen-Ninety-Three

May or some bullshit it seemed

Another moment in youth gone south

Waiting to head out the door

Off to Dodge

He was a little older than me

The Boat Man

He loved his own voice

Was bragging how he would just roll in

Hook up

Another ship to the big city

Nice paycheck

He was a funny cat

Came from the same neighborhood

We got tight

Mainly played spades

Wishing we had some cigs

It was just a bright idea

How to get a cig in this fucking place

Thor Jr

Looked like he just walked off a ship

That sailed from Valhalla to Earth

Reality

Inside for beating a stripper

Got his package

After his first week, in

Fucking deodorant and toothpaste

Toothpaste

What a remarkable thing

"Who sent you the toothpaste?"

His sister

How nice

Collect call to my buddy

This is a collect call from you know who

Do you accept the charges?

Of course

Hey man, can ya do me a solid?

"Anything, name it!"

Go buy a box of toothpaste

Take a razor blade

Open the box at the end

That simple place where its glued

It can't be torn

Be careful, use delicacy

Has to be perfect

Eject some of the paste

Take some large straws

Fold one end

Melt it with a lighter

Take a cig

Remove the filter

Stick them in

Melt the other end

Get as many as you can to fit

Put the tube back into the box

Glue the end shut

Just like factory

I can hear him writing the shit down

"Got it, do I drop it off?"

No, send it via mail!

"Done."

Thanks a bunch

The Boat Man does the same

One week to the day

A package in thy name

Toothpaste

Box opened and inspected

Jailor hands me my new-found love

Into my cell

Four straws

Nine cigs

Like gold upon the fingers

Only problem

How the fuck we going to light them

Great, the exclamation point above the brain

The pencil

Lead #2 comes into play

For the fuck who paid attention in Science

With teeth

Peel the wood away

Till only one large piece of lead remains

Conductor of Electricity

Unplug the community boob tube

Break off three pieces of lead

Two into the outlet

One on each side

Other wrapped around some tissue

Time to partake in the fun

Down it goes

Beautiful the sound

Like a vicious Grrr

Arching sparks

The flame comes to life

An Olympian in an instant

Running into the cell

Lighting the cigarette

Five inmates:

The Boat man, decided it's fun to steal mini yachts

Thor Jr, took it upon himself to beat a stripper down

The Mexican, drunk driving, those awesome Mothers!

Broken Wing that awesome Native American

Beating an officer of the law into oblivion

Myself, thief extraordinaire

Hence, why I was in Jail like an idiot

Standing around a toilet

Flushing the smoke away

The greatest piece of heaven

Cigarettes

How the hell we going to do this better

The Mexican

Ingenious idea

One book of matches

Remove the matches

Cut off the striker

Into the straw

Five guys in a cube

Everybody getting toothpaste

Jailer on first shift

"Y'all get a lot of toothpaste, you eating the shit?"

It was almost in unison

"No, we all just want clean teeth!"

Smoking in Jail

Our norm

Time came and went

The Boat Man

He was sent up river

Gave me his smokes

"They have Cigs in the joint!"

Take care, don't let Bubba pack ya ass!

Smiles

The Mexican released next

He was the coolest of shits

Though English, he barely spoke a lick

Broken Wing off to the big house

He just gave me the finger while he smiled

Thor Jr and myself

All that remained in cell block A

My turn

Time to run off to Dodge

I just whistled the song

They call us problem child

We spend our lives on trial

I never laid eyes on them again

Though, the smoking in jail

Something I'll never forget

Best fucking time

Never laughing so hard

Lighting ass wipe on fire

Five clowns blowing smoke down a toilet

Priceless

I fucking love that my life has been a remarkable journey worthy of a shitty story

Excellent Productions

A behind the scenes look at the number one rated program

ITS ON

with

Fox Flowgasmic

INSIDE THE PRODUCTION BOOTH

Cue Music

Cue Lights

Camera Three Pan out

Cue the Host

Host walks out

Camera one zoom in

Cue Teleprompter

Host

Reading from the teleprompter

Good evening Cocksuckers and Crotch-crickets

This is Fox Flowgasmic

Cause you parasites didn't already know this

Jesus Christ, are you serious?

Every damn time it's this shit

For fucks sake Janet

Can't we get a better introduction?

Tim, ya dumb cunt

Is my intercom on?

What button?

I don't see a fucking button

Don't talk to me you prick, just turn it on

Christ, every day the help just gets worse and worse

****BEEP****

Janet, ya dumb box!

How many times do I need to address this?

****BUZZ****

"Fox, you will read what is on the screen! Christ, do you believe this guy?"

****BEEP****

I heard that Janet and let me remind you that I am the "SHOW"!

****BUZZ****

"Of Course, you are Fox."

****BEEP****

Janet, write me up something other than this regurgitated garbage

Shit, can we fire this worthless writer!

Gocni Schindler couldn't write his way out of a box.

Get some awesome talented bimbo in here

Bringing another dick tingling epidemic

To the Universal News Show

Cue the god damn Laughter

****BUZZ****

Do not cue laughter, Fox, we need to get this wrapped up to make the deadline, we can surely address this another time. Please read from the script

****PLACES EVERYONE****

RETAKE

Cue Music

Cue Lights

Cue the Host

Host walks out

Cue Teleprompter

Host

Reading from the teleprompter

Good evening Ladies and Gents

This is Fox Flowgasmic

On the number one broadcasted program on

Planet earth

Welcome to

IT'S ON

What's on?

Whoa, ah, have we got a show for you

We have one hell of a guest

Whoa, ah

He is the LARGER than LIFE interweb bully

Whoa, ah that's right

The one and only who

Single handedly broken homes

Stolen hearts

Beaten souls

Leaving a trail of waste

Whoa

Ah

I introduce you to the great Silver Back

The ape

Cyberbully Joel Extraordinaire

****APPLAUSE-APPLAUSE-APPLAUSE****

Whoa, yes, yes

Here he is everyone

****SCREAMS-SHOUTING-SCREAMS****

Yes, whoa, ah

How you doing brother?

"Excellent ya douche!"

"LAUGHTER"

****LAUGH-APPLAUSE-LAUGH****

Cue Pyro

The stage explodes into a fiery ball of hells inferno

Host and Guest sit down

Cue Exhaust

Cue Commercial

Go Commercial

**** Thirty Seconds Everyone ****

****BEEP****

Janet, what cesspool did you drag this vagina out from?

****BUZZ****

He's got over Fifty Million Scum Tube Subscribers! This guy is going to be the death of me!

****BEEP****

I heard that Janet

****TEN SECONDS****
Positions everyone

Cue lights

Three, two, one

GO

Welcome back

Now Joel, is there any truth that you make a living by badgering and assaulting innocent people just trying to get by on social media?

Joel scratching his bald head

"Are you allowed to say Assaulting on the television Fox?"

This is propaganda media program Joel; I'll say whatever the fuck I want. In these times, everyone's vagina's bleeds red!

So, you assault people then?

"Assault people Fox! I set them up with simple questions. Snares for them to step in, then, I unleash my verbal slaughter. So, if you want to label it an assault. I guess if that's the crime, then I'm guilty as hell.

Interesting, so I see that you have a video on Scum Tube. Where you clearly brag about breaking up over three hundred marriages. We have a real Don Juan here ladies and gents, and gents lock up your wives.

****LAUGHTER-LAUGHTER-LAUGHTER****

"Actually Fox, that is a correct fact, I have conversations and the photos to prove it!"

Oh, really, you don't say, you don't say!

"Ya callin me a liar Fox?"

Cue Camera 2 Zoom in on Joel Angry face

Goodness, no Joel, just asking the questions.

"I was about ready to blast you in that cock hole Fox, help wipe off that two-dollar smirk on your fucking face!"

INSIDE THE PRODUCTION BOOTH

Cue Camera Three zoom in on Fox

"Janet, Fox looks like he is going to piss his pants!"

God, I hope so, just keep rolling!

Camera Two pan in

ON STAGE

Ha-ha, now Joel, no need to revert to violence, after all, the world is watching.

"I don't give a shit who is watching, you think this is funny?"

"Am I funny Fox?!?"

Whoa, ah, um, ah, whoa well shit!

Joel comes in close to Fox

"What's wrong maggot, cat got your tongue? I'm sorry I'm not one of these little bitches in front row hoping to give you a blow after the show stroking that ass hole ego! You wanted the real deal, well here I am mother fucker. Now, to answer your shit question with some facts. No, I didn't break up the marriages. These dumb boxes who are married, decided to talk to a real man. I just played along.

Within seconds, I'm getting videos and pics of tits and ass. I wanted to see the result of sending them to their husbands.

Heading titled

"Look at your wife!"

Fox grimaces a bit

Whoa, ah, so you told the husband? Doesn't that make you a bit of a cunt?

The audience laughs

"Oh, this is entertaining! Fox your stupidity is keeping me on the edge of my seat."

Fox perplexed

Edge of your seat, how so Joel?

Cracking his knuckles

"Cause Fox, I so want to shove this fist into your skull"

****LAUGHTER-LAUGHTER-LAUGHTER****

Cue HOST

Cue Commercial Break

Ha-ha you're a funny guy Joel, please don't go anywhere Folks, we will be back after a few words from our sponsors.

Go Commercial

****SIXTY SECONDS EVERYBODY****

****BEEP****

Janet, what the hell is going on here?

****BUZZ****

Looks like this guy knows you, might want to try a different approach

****BEEP****

A different approach, the guy is like a walking time bomb.

****BUZZ****

This isn't the kind of talk from the man that ""is the show"". Put your big boy panties on and figure it out. Shit, I have twenty that Fox gets choked out. Laughter fills the production box.

****BEEP****

I heard that Janet! Bitch...

****TEN SECONDS****

Cue lights

Three, two, one

GO

BACK ON STAGE

Welcome back

So now Joel, what was the initial response you'd typically find yourself receiving from the husbands?

Joel smashing his fists together

"Typical response, Oh, I don't know Fox, I received mainly a thank you. I mean, I just saved some cocksucker from a possible living hell"

Fox raises his left eyebrow

Do you really feel you "Saved Them"?

Joel angered

"Of course, I saved them. Ya know, I don't really like you Fox!'

Fox smirks

Oh, why don't you like me Joel?

Joel grinding his teeth

"You're a whimpering little bitch, Yeah, I heard you on the intercom. You must think I'm stupid?"

Fox sits back looking up at the booth

I don't think your stupid, you are a cunt, not stupid

Joel laughing

"Ya know Fox, I was on your social media page, you have eight hundred thousand and change of human parasites that have given you likes! Some fucks to give air to that ego"

Fox holding his head up

Ha-ha, Yeah, something like that

Joel gets in Fox's face

"Fox, you're Pathetic! Ya put on a show for some wrinkled old hag to watch while her husband is pinching one off to some porn while on the shitter! I have over five million likes; you really should be my little bitch."

Attempting to divert Joel's rage

Whoa, ah, this isn't about who has what, this is about this interview Joel

Smirking

"Well, it sure the hell is, seems I have broader fan base than some washed up ass that just wants his ego stroked by some box named Janet."

An angered Fox

Joel, you're a little out of line now

Laughing obnoxiously loud

"I'm not out of line, I'm right on point

Fox reading the notes from the teleprompter

Now Joel, we've been informed that a death occurred from something you posted about another person care to elaborate on this.

Adjusting his cock

"yeah, the DA thought he could catch me a case because some little cry baby couldn't handle the burn. Shit isn't my problem that the loser couldn't decipher from make-believe to reality."

Studying Joel's body language

Whoa, ah, so you don't think your words have an impact?

Leaning in towards Fox

"Of course, my words have an impact, I'm damn near a god!"

Fox abrupt in laughter

You're no god Joel

The audience laughs

Clenching fists

"Calling me a liar again Fox? Not nice! Say, what type of tie is that?"

Looking down then lifting the colored tie with his hand

Its silk, very expensive

With a sincere genuine expression

"Can I feel it?"

Contemplating the thought

Odd request, sure, why not.

Big hands take hold

"My, that is soft, must have cost a small fortune?"

Looking down Fox perceives the eyes of a man who believes himself to be a god.

Whoa, ah, um, ha-ha, half a day's pay for me, a month's salary for you.

Strong hands grip

"See, there you go again!"

Joel proceeds to choke Fox with his own tie

Everything captured on camera

INSIDE THE PRODUCTION BOOTH

"Janet, should I call security?"

Not yet fool, I need Fox to turn blue! This is going to boost ratings through the roof.

"Janet, he is going to kill Fox!"

Alright, but keep recording, I want all of this. We will finally get the attention this show has been needing for years.

"Security is on its way!"

Look at that ass hole Fox down there, squirming around, begging for his life like some dog. Oh, that reminds me,

> pay up!

"Where did you find this guy Janet?"

Prison, the warden owed me a solid, we made up the story

"What?!? Why?"

The show has been sinking for years, needed something drastic to save it

"Did Fox know this?"

Hell no, that's what makes it real!

"Security is here."

Christ, he is dragging Fox around like some rag doll

"Fox is definitely blue."

Perfect

Camera Two

Get up on Fox, I want to see his face in agony

"Janet, look at that, they Shocked Joel and it also went into Fox"

Christ, he's salivating at the mouth, jerking, like fresh roadkill.

"They're dragging Joel away. Fox is rolling over; seems he is going to be OK!"

****BUZZ****

Fox, you there?

****BUZZ****

Fox

****BUZZ****

FOX!!

One small, frail hand, reaches up attempting to grab the intercom

Failing the first, second, third and fourth try

Fifth was the charm

****BEEP****

Janet, bitch, I could have been killed

****BUZZ****

Quit crying , pull yourself together Fox and finish the show.

****BEEP****

Janet, this is my middle finger do you see it?

****BUZZ****

Yes, Fox, we got it

****BEEP****

This is Fox Flowgasmic

Host of

IT'S ON

Signing the fuck off

Janet, Suck my cock!

Joel went back to prison
Fox was a guest on Good Hell America
Janet received a promotion

All she wanted was my money

She manipulated her way to get it

I just gave it freely

Only way she'd get the hell away from me

I Still Write

I was told I need to twitter

Then snappy some instaspamy

Send them a SnapChatter

Give them a Viney

Well, I need to finish my second book.

Can't do that living on this social media

No twatter for me

No Instagrammy

No Snap&see

No teleMe

No videoviney

no, no, NO!

God, dammit, I'm a human Being!

There is no direct result to anything

Though, I still believe in old school ways

Do good

Hope for the success of others

Help people

Word of mouth, still seems to be the best route

Fuck Amazon and its .99 cents

It's funny

I was reading some ravings for a number one book.

One of those chick books

Love me lots of Gar'Be nice Gocni!"

Then, I read about the author

Came from the rich side of the hood!

Success, via inherited bank roll

Happy for the damn writer

It was still work I'm sure.

Though, it does help

When you have a good amount of money

Don't have some ball buster boss to deal with

Bills are paid

Comfort of a secluded home

Not like this

Not ten kids screaming across the paper wall

In this rented room

Don't leave the clothes on the floor

Roaches man, roaches!

Jesus, does the noise ever stop?

Fuck me

Nope, just some money to live on worry free

To toss at promoting

Then you can hire someone

To do all this Instagrammy

Twatting about while on the teleMe!

P.S you can also buy a really, great Editor!

Like Bill T good

When you have some money,

Tt just makes life that much easier.

I'm a poetry wrangler

It means I'm broke

The kind of value

That is written inside a toilet stall

"You Get Paid for that?"

No I haven't gotten paid yet

"I was going to say, I get that FOR FREE while visiting the shitter!!!"

Yeah, it makes sense you'd take it for free

Dullard discouraging me, how dare he

Comparing me to a fucking latrine

What blessings

I still write though

Fuck'em if my words don't include a dick pic

Or some nude chick

Some Professional baller

Free-lance photographer

Toby that drug dog

A killer Gnome running the halls

Wealthy prick sweeping little miss nothing off her feet

Telling his pals, he went slummin

Some ass hole, in his yacht

Wearing that doucher hat and aviators

Hey, ass hole, you haven't even left port.

Yeah, fuck you too!

I still write

Don't really give a fuck

Have another beer

I'd like some dope instead

That's illegal here

Well doesn't here just suck

This stress

Is like climbing a fucking mountain of pebbles.

Each attempt, only fills my damn shoes

Sends me rolling back to the bottom.

There must be an easier way

There is Gocni!

There is?

"Yes, it's quite simple"

Please tell me?

"It's simple"

Yeah, OK!

"No, it's super simple"

Hmmm, sounds familiar

Almost like I read that before!

"Simple! Really, really simple"

That's so awesome that it's simple! What is it?

"Simply just sell your book"

Oh, just simply sell my book!

"Simple, isn't it?"

Just a sec let me grab something

"Simply take your time"

Oh, I will!

"Hey, what's the hammer for?"

Simply going to bash your brains in!

"Ah, no Gocni, Bad, bad Gocni"

Its simple math really, you take this like a simple man!

"I don't want to die"

Well it's simple I hit you like this and like that

Ugh, thud_____

See how simple that was!

Oh, hi, I simply didn't see you reading this

Sorry about that

What did you say?

One Eighty-Seven

Really wasn't a one eighty-seven

Just a couple of friends simply banging it out

No, goodness, you don't need to call the police

It was simply just a misunderstanding

Yeah, he looks way worse than what he actually is

No, he's fine, let me show you

See he's doing great

No, I didn't move his hand and speak for him

You simply saw me do what?

No, he doesn't need an ambulance

Skull fracture! No, he's hardly bleeding

That blood was simply there before all of this

Oh, come on, you're dialing Nine-One-One

Hey, can you do me a solid?

I know you're on the phone with the Officers

It will simply take a minute

Thanks a bunch

Yeah, just hold this hammer for a sec

Great, you're simply the best!

Where am, I going?

Wait here for the police?

No, I have to run and get some Ice

I'll be back in a jiffy!

Yeah, hold his head up please

No, don't drop the hammer

You need to wave that at the police!

Why?

Christ, so they know you have the tool!

Listen, time is just simply being wasted

This guy really needs the ice

Be back with the quickness!

Thanks

More waste! God dammit Gocni.

Drink My Sour Milk

A message beacons

On one of those, giant light up arrows

The kind they use at the strip clubs

Naked Bitches & Kick Ass Liquor

Message on this sign

Nothing of the like

Liars Are Fryers

That's the message

Going to fry

Fry for being a fucking liar!

Fry mother fuckers, fry

Living this lie on the daily

Fry

Life as it is

This one being

Out of billions

Blasting normalcy away

Signed up servant

Waving my sackless flag

Indebted slave, hell yeah

An Illuminated anal rape volunteer

After another Twelver on the clock

Sleeping in a borrowed home

Simply watching broke man's entertainment

My flat screen

This Fruit Cake

Proclaiming how insignificant

We truly are

In THE scope of "EVERYTHING"

WOW, FAR THE FUCK OUT!

Keeps saying that shit

"Wow, far out."

Proclaiming it repeatedly!

Just how absolutely minute in scope we are

His words, obviously pointless

Who are these "entertainers"

Feeling entitled enough

Attempting to dictate who or what

Let alone

The sack size to speak for all mankind

Enter the tale of the two broads

Bridget and Jenny

Went to see the

"ROCKSTAR"

Who speaks for all

Jenny is trying to view over heads of people

Poopisnickles Bridget, the damn line is for miles

Like, it will take forever to see him!

Bridgett standing with crossed legs

Like, I'm not waiting in line to like see the Rockstar!

Like, I have to like, pee and all

Jenny jumps up and down

Throwing some form of tantrum

Like it's our only shot at this

like you must stay with me, you have too!

Bridgett shaking

Like Jenny, hello, like I'm going to piss my pants

Jenny doesn't give a fuck!

She wants to blow the "ROCKSTAR"

Bridgett bouncing in agony

Like Jenny, help me!

Jenny is long gone in mind

Bridgett pissed her pants

Yeah, we have them

Those who would just repeat

That same form of gibberish

"Yeah, I'm insignificant in life, Fruit Cake said so!"

You have a question!

What's that?

Oh, what was with Bridgett and Jenny thing?

Nothing, Bridgett pissed her pants

Jenny's a slut, it's what she likes

So, as I was sayin

These free floaters

Getting a peace sign

Tattooed on their foreheads

Waving at nothing

While dancing air

It's not LsD

Those who fool heartedly

Chase the kite off thousand-foot cliff

Well shit, they should have grown wings

You'd think

I mean logically

Eventually, one of them would grow wings

Where is evolution when ya need it most?

Myself no

I don't feel small in scope

Yet, this Fruit Cake clown ass sniffer

With some infinite wisdom

Is selling an answer

He's a man, man has no answers

He's selling the illusion for $19.95

Enter Bob the fat fuck

"Oh, "blahuhuha" Now, come Gocni, Man has done a lot!"

Oh, like what?

"Well, huH, WE HAVE, we have, TECHNOLOGY!!"

Yeah, it's great.

Connected the world, made it smaller.

Also, disconnected us from each other.

Now what we got?

All we have is a picture with words

Inside a glass display

Can't go anywhere,

Without some broad

Snappin a selfie

Fish lips, we need more fish lips god dammit!

Almost like a zombie apocalypse

Except, the people!

Yeah, the people, are still breathing, still alive Bob!

Technology is great, it will also be man's demise!

Bobs scratches his hairy sasquatch ass

"Now, now, Gocni, that's a bit harsh, after all, you use it!"

I sure do!

I love it, best thing to ever happen.

I also love cigarettes

Love riding a motorcycle

Like pounding down Alcohol

Enjoy Mary Jane

Never once, did I proclaim, to be some, role model

This shit isn't Disney on Ice

Hey kids, for nineteen ninety-nine

You too can become the Official

Buckaroo Gocni Gang Bangers Ranger

Quick kids, go tells your parents

Even if it's four A.M on the West Coast

Go wake them up

Give them a good closed fist

That usually does the trick

Shove that cock sucking iPad into their throats

Screw it just purchase it

It will be OK

Our little secret

(Gocni, Psst, Gocni you can't say that!)

Shit, I forgot this was confession

The priest wants some head

Mary can wait her turn

Piss off dude in a booth

Kids

Make them parents purchase

Now remember

Download the app

Purchase it immediately

What's that Jeff?

The first fifty callers get what

What's this?

No Way!!

First fifty callers

Are getting the "MAGIC BELT"!!

Say what, no way!

(CUE EXCITEMENT: THESE ASS HOLES NEED TO PURCHASE)

Hurry up kids

I'm so excited!

Don't forget, Subscribe to my ShitTube

Hey, follow me on twatter, Tweet! So, cute! I know!

No! None of that shit for this guy

I'm no damn role model

The shit is just laid out there in the open

Amazes me

How mindlessly humans don't notice

Just part of the problem

Not like it will ever go away

It's going to get worse

Much Worse

One dude staring at the ground

There, right there, do you see it?

"What am I supposed to see?"

That grid, you don't see it?

"No man, you're kinda freakin me out a little, brah"

You seriously don't see the grid?

"No man, you alright? Do I need to call someone?"

No all good

He couldn't see it

Kinda like I couldn't see the sailboat

Shit, my Mallrats

It so obvious

Accepted, like swiping my American Ass

This stupid chip bullshit!

Nothing was wrong with swiping

I'm hoarding cash now

When they eliminate it

Will have value as collectors' items

"That is part of change son!"

Well, what about the Gung-ho attitude

You remember, Don't you?

Went like this

We'll, that's how dad did it

And well, gosh damn it!

That's how we're gonna do it!

This asshole said
Ahh shit!
Where was I going with this again?
"What's wrong stupid, Cat's got your brain?
(Cue Laughter)

Shut it, now's not the time for this!

"Seems the perfect time for retard to forget the story!"

Glad someone found their ass hole card.

"Never leave home without it!"

Yeah! Great, now piss off!

"I'm going to kill you, buttermilk, you'll be nothing!"

It's great to still be breathing air at nothing

"I'm serious wise ass"

This shit is the best you got?

Get the fuck out of here loser!!

What a tool

OH, my dear.

Hey you, the reader!

Yeah you!

Great, thanks, hey pay no mind to that.

Just that voice that is always there

(Cue Tears)

Sometimes, oh god, is just too much

(Cue Sobbing)

Oh, what's that?

You Sympathize!

That's really sweet

So, take the rope off my neck

Like this?

Thumbs up!

Great, I did it correctly

Shaking your head for yes

Looks like hanging myself is out of the question

I wish I could look at the look on your beautiful mug

Sitting here, there on the shitter, hopefully

Reading, this side of amazing, while droppin a stinker

"Is this guy, is this guy really talking about hanging himself?"

(CUE LAUGHTER)

Obviously, I was

FYI

It is all real!

Get fucked up

Drink all that Vodka for pussies

Smoke it

Take this pill

Swallow, swallow it now

Inject this

No, inject it!

Numb this world away

Drink my sour milk

Liars are Fryers

So, the message said

Weld it Better

I used to work for this fab shop

Upper Midwest

Everyone talked like drunken sailors

It was f this and f that

Shit, hell, Bob and Buddy

Attempting to do my best

Welding away as a logical number

The old timers giving me grief

Always riding me

"What in the fuck are you doing young Buck?!?"

Welding

"You call that shit a weld?"

Yeah, several passes

"Boy, you better cut that out and do it over!"

What, there is nothing wrong with it

"Look at all that undercut."

What undercut?

"That right there, just wait till Lowel sees this shit!"

There is nothing wrong with it

"OK, I warned you, Lowel is going to write you up."

What the hell did I do?

I cut it out and welded it again

Fucking Old Timers laughing behind the LVD

"Stupid new kid, cutting out a perfectly good weld!"

Yeah, the shit I had to deal with

I was naive and got smart

Was nice when I could understand good bullshit

It's really a language

It's really a fine art

Lowel, was an ass hole!

Fucking guy, constantly turn my radio down

He did it when I was in the middle of a weld

Once you begin, you go to completion

Can't stand bullshit starts and stops

The prick enjoyed it

Bastard would take it away

My only pleasure

Fucking radio wars, the excuse he would give

Knowing full well

I had to endure the silence

Those mundane noises from grinders

Welders cracking the arch

Shit Press Brakes

Lowel, sitting there

Reveling in my misery

Sometimes, my fellow inmates

Oops, no, not inmates

Just number slaves

Pulling the Lowel card

Sneak in and turn it down

Then, like a fool, I'd go and bitch to them about it

Monkeys getting their enjoyment

Loving the moments

I would learn to love it as well

It was a job

Just something I showed up for

Though, my spirit was being slaughtered

I wanted something more

This truly can't be all there is in life?

Can it?

Please, tell me there is more!

Going into a place

That feels more like a tomb

Those Old Timers

Mentors from a different world

It was an enjoyment working with them

Really, the only enjoyment I had

I loved welding

Building from nothing

Truly an artistic craft

I just couldn't be the number

Weld looking into a mirror

Use the extended horse cock

Then one winter

Things would change

Scratch that

Start to change

This cat who worked across from me

Fell on the ice

Hurt his hip pretty bad.

"Ahh, it will get better boy!"

He was sorta positive, ya know!

It didn't get better

One day, he didn't show up for work

This guy never missed a day

Always, always working all the OT

Day after next, he was dead

Had cancer

No farewell

Nothing, he was just dead

New guy to take his place

Didn't even know it

It impacted me deeply

Spending this life

Doing this

Barely making the bills

Unless you do the OT

All of it

Shortly after all this

I too would meet cancer head on

Wasn't me, it was my own flesh and blood.

Soon all of that would be gone

Life is like that

Taking a journey into the dark

Holding a one inch candle stick

Wishing for the best

Don't get me wrong

I had everything you could ever dream

A beautiful house

Water view from afar

A wife and title

Yet, in this everything, I had nothing

It was simplistic complacency

Not one thing wrong with that

Some people love this notion

Hell, I thought it was for me

Maybe, before death it was

Sorry, that would be a lie

I just couldn't live it anymore

She has a name, I don't call her ex

That's just disrespectful

I remember, I loved this woman once

Still, do I love her I suppose

Not though, in any romantic sense

That left with respect

Suicided itself out some window

I find her annoying though

Realistic reality

We grew to our own conditioning

Apart!

We never really seen it

Was just another part of the process

I'm not into holding people back either

This time, on earth, is very limited

One moment ago, I was twenty

Now up in age

Wandering Jimmy, where did the time go?

Since then, I've been place to place

Discovered a good part of America

I have zero interest in Europe

Can't have been too great if my ancestry

Left the damn place

No, I love America, for I am American

Still, much to explore in this amazing country

I don't own much

Coming from having it all

Currently, not much of anything

My stress isn't high in level

Waking with a smile is a blessing

Yet, I find myself, also, incomplete.

Like seeing this age

With nothing to show

Except, a motorcycle

Some Ross for Less clothes

Memorabilia saved from a time long ago

A bank account reflecting this guy doesn't have shit

I'm still grateful

Appreciative for life

Getting my shit together

Has been a work in progress

Getting a life together

What is together?

Is having a life "together" owning all the best of things?

I don't know

Writing is what makes me rich

Not in no material sense

Hell, if money was my cause

There would be no poetry

Each one of these

Part of this walk

Took time to write

Think about

Paid a price at gaining the experience

Doing shit with this life

Partaking in the world

Like some drunken fisherman

Hooking his chum

Tossing me out into the vastness

Time to catch some giant fish

That no one will ever see

I'll be the good bait

Catching the greatest of beasts

It was always my dream

To be the best

Twelve years of me

Into a place, I was never meant

Though, it was my complacency

That settled me

A great fear

What if I lose it all?

So, this would-be life

Weld it Better

The Old Timer would scream

Weld it Better

No, that's not my life though

I miss those guys

Old Timers

The funny pranks

Great the stories

My art of welding

I'm just bigger than being a number

My eyes perceive stars

I no longer want to look at rocks under my feet

Life is meant to be lived

Not held back by ideas

Getting a life together

My life is together

Welded better!

Take what you can use

Leave nothing to waste

For Fucks sake, help someone in need

Quit with living life

In a selfish means

It holds no rewards

But "look at me"!

I don't feel right about being here
My spirit doesn't belong in this time zone
I endure this hell
Courage prevents me from ending this damnation
I somehow... prevail

Raise some Hell

It was just another doucher event

Bunch of chest banger's

Knuckle draggin some beautiful broads

Obviously, the rocks fell out a long time ago

But hey, we're not going to talk about this

That story is lame

Shit, Its gay

"Oh, my God Elizabeth, he said "GAY" he's a fucking racist!"

Beth, another Beth

Beth, I'll pull out my racism for you to suck

ZIP

I said gay,

I'll say it again

Gay

Now crawl back out from that cow's vagina

"You know Janet, this Gocni really upsets my feelings!"

Great, let's talk about them feelings

In another damn life, of course

After some alien archaeologist pulls my skull

From some hole in the earth

Then, and only then

Can we talk about "FEELINGS"?

Screw Dr. Phil

Grow a pair

Go to a Midwest bar

Partake in that style of tale

Faggots

"OMG he said, FAGGOTS!!! Let's Crucify!"

Stop being so sensitive

This ordeal is the story?

No, we're going to take a little trip

The time

It doesn't matter

Some wild kids

A whole pack of them

Doing shit, the good kids didn't do

Hooligans

Amongst us was an instigator

Always attempting to get two of us to fight each other

"Dude said he was going to kick your ass!"

Normal kid listening skills

Oh yeah, fuck that guy

Typical dumb shit like that

Next thing, you're getting blindsided by a right hook

Rolling on the ground

Getting muddy

Becoming bloody

For nothing

Another time, it was a knife fight

We really didn't mess around

Shocked, surprised none of us died

The way we were in the neighborhood

We ran the river

Owned the town

The younger kid

Apparently bolder, even told the cops

"I own this town!"

The cops just looked at one another

You own it do you!

"Yeah, I own it!"

They dropped him on the outside of town

Twenty mile walk back

Yeah, it was owned

We had a place to fight

A location to fish

The boards over the river

Moms would always scream

"Never, ever swim in that river!"

Just walking out, the door

Yes, mom, I won't, I PROMISE!

Bullshit really

Swam in it every day I could

Come home smelling like it

Mom bitching

"You little mother fucker, you were swimming in the river?"

Giving it the old sincere attempt

No mom, I wasn't, I SWEAR

It was amateur hour

In the lying department

"Don't you lie to me you little fucker, think I was born yesterday!"

For some idiotic reason

Delusions crept in

Thinking I would get away with it

No mom, I didn't, SCOUTS HONOR

"You ain't no boy scout Gocni Asher Schindler!"

The conclusion

Loss of privileges

Big time whooping

Every whip from the belt

"I told you little fucker, NO!"

Every blast

My ass bouncing all over the place

Trying not to laugh

If that came out

Would turn into a whole new level of death

Lasted a few days

Back to the river

Returning to raise some hell

Looking back

To a time that feels like yesterday

Though now, it's a billion miles from me

Childhood friends

A good portion of them dead

Boards fell into the river

Mighty the tree

No competition for a river roaring free

At this current moment

In an age of understanding

I was an idiot for swimming in that

Though in youth

Somehow, god damned invincible

Now, I'd probably bust a hip

The area once had orchards

It was a war zone

Nothing finer than bouncing a Cortland

Off one of those ass hole friend's heads

Till the farmer started shootin

His Rock salt gun at us wild hooligans

"Get outta my orchard ya lil sons-a-bitches!"

It was always an enjoyment hitching rides on trains

Heading off to the bigger city

Skateboarding

Getting chased by the police

No Skateboarding on the sidewalk

Skateboarders keep out

We Tolerate no Skateboarding on these premises

Always fun to break those rules

Down the parking ramps

Through the mall

Treated like some plague

Those naughty ones

Never following the rules

Love the fact I lived a childhood

A real Huck Finn

Screw the parasitic fools

Wanting to conform us

Guess seeing society as a joke

Has always been there!

We always played the wild card

It was bullying

Beatings

Best of times

It's why I'm not a pussy in life

Take my licks

Keep on a steppin

Don't give a fuck

Here is the middle finger

We owned this town

Least that side of the river

Preacher left us on the curb

Lived for raising hell

Not getting brainwashed with lies

Some trash, spewing out of some teacher's black hole

Regrets I have no problem with

Just as long as I never regret living this experience

Fuck it

Sometimes you need to raise a little hell

Let lose those inner cravings

Back to some beast land

But We're not talking about

Cavemen in the land of broads

That book is shit!

This Concludes the book

Thanks for reading and supporting my ass!

PEACE OUT!

Bonus Story

Camaro Driving

I drove my Camaro hard
She was losing her shit in the passenger seat
I just wanted her gone
She opened the door
I watched in amazement
She placed her feet to moving ground
I smiled
She screamed
I gazed to a spinning human being
She wasn't moving
I kept on rollin
Farewell to bipolar
Farewell psychotic
Couple month's pass
She emailed an ultrasound
Selling me a pregnancy
I laughed
Its missing the date
She emailed a grave marker
Said she had a miscarry
I sent back
How convenient

Once upon a time in the universe
There was this big deity
Out walking around
One day, he had the shits
Earth looked good a place as any
Low and behold
Humanity, somehow, slithered
This concludes Religion and Evolution
Coexisting.

Made in the USA
Las Vegas, NV
27 June 2021